Thoughts and Notes at Home and Abroad

Elihu Burritt

CAMBRIDGE
UNIVERSITY PRESS

CAMBRIDGE UNIVERSITY PRESS

Cambridge, New York, Melbourne, Madrid, Cape Town,
Singapore, São Paolo, Delhi, Tokyo, Mexico City

Published in the United States of America by Cambridge University Press, New York

www.cambridge.org
Information on this title: www.cambridge.org/9781108032650

© in this compilation Cambridge University Press 2011

This edition first published 1868
This digitally printed version 2011

ISBN 978-1-108-03265-0 Paperback

CAMBRIDGE LIBRARY COLLECTION

Books of enduring scholarly value

Literary Studies

This series provides a high-quality selection of early printings of literary works, textual editions, anthologies and literary criticism which are of lasting scholarly interest. Ranging from Old English to Shakespeare to early twentieth-century work from around the world, these books offer a valuable resource for scholars in reception history, textual editing, and literary studies.

Thoughts and Notes at Home and Abroad

American philanthropist Elihu Burritt (1810–79) was involved in and lectured widely on many causes, including the abolition of slavery, temperance, and world peace. Known as the 'learned blacksmith' because of his early training in the trade, he was eventually appointed US consul in Birmingham, England, from 1865 to 1870. In addition to his campaigning, Burritt was a prolific writer, producing books and articles on a range of subjects. In this work, published in 1868, he assembles a collection of his writings published between 1850 and 1855 in a variety of periodicals. This compilation covers a wide range of topics – from the Great Exhibition of 1851 to the 'Anarchy of Governments' – drawing from his experiences in Europe and in the USA. Much of Burritt's writing is devoted to the issue of international relations, and to his desire for a 'Congress of Nations' devoted to ending conflict in Europe.

Cambridge University Press has long been a pioneer in the reissuing of out-of-print titles from its own backlist, producing digital reprints of books that are still sought after by scholars and students but could not be reprinted economically using traditional technology. The Cambridge Library Collection extends this activity to a wider range of books which are still of importance to researchers and professionals, either for the source material they contain, or as landmarks in the history of their academic discipline.

Drawing from the world-renowned collections in the Cambridge University Library, and guided by the advice of experts in each subject area, Cambridge University Press is using state-of-the-art scanning machines in its own Printing House to capture the content of each book selected for inclusion. The files are processed to give a consistently clear, crisp image, and the books finished to the high quality standard for which the Press is recognised around the world. The latest print-on-demand technology ensures that the books will remain available indefinitely, and that orders for single or multiple copies can quickly be supplied.

The Cambridge Library Collection will bring back to life books of enduring scholarly value (including out-of-copyright works originally issued by other publishers) across a wide range of disciplines in the humanities and social sciences and in science and technology.

THOUGHTS AND NOTES

AT

HOME AND ABROAD.

THOUGHTS AND NOTES

AT

HOME AND ABROAD.

BY

ELIHU BURRITT.

LONDON:

CASSELL, PETTER, AND GALPIN.

AND 596, BROADWAY, NEW YORK.

1868.

Printed by *Joſiah Allen*, jun., Birmingham.

PREFACE.

THE author would respectfully submit a few facts and observations to the readers of this volume, to explain its character and objects, and the reason of its appearance. In the year 1844 he commenced the publication of a weekly newspaper in Worcester, Mass., called "The Christian Citizen." It was especially devoted to the Anti-Slavery cause, Peace, Temperance, and Self-Cultivation. In 1846 he first visited England, where he remained three years; still continuing his paper in Massachusetts. During this sojourn in the Mother Country, he originated several enterprises for the promotion of peace and friendly intercourse and fraternal sympathy between different countries. One of these was an association called "The League of Universal Brotherhood," which numbered at one time ten thousand members in Great Britain and as many in the United States. The practical objects and labours of this association were the promotion of international Peace Congresses, International Friendly Addresses, Ocean Penny Postage, encouragement of Free Labour in slave-holding countries, and other enterprises of similar spirit. One of the most interesting and useful of them was called "The Olive Leaf Mission." This was the monthly insertion in about forty continental journals of a column of short articles and paragraphs on the subject of peace, extracted from the speeches and writings of eminent men of different countries. This column was called an "Olive Leaf for the People;" and it appeared monthly in newspapers printed in seven different languages, from Madrid to St. Petersburgh, and from Stockholm to Vienna. The whole sum paid to all these journals for the publication of the "Olive Leaf" was about £300 a year. This amount was contributed by the ladies of the United Kingdom, who formed over a hundred associations for this purpose, called "Olive Leaf Societies," all of which were organized under the personal direction or suggestion of the author, who was present to explain the objects of the under-taking.

In connexion with the Ocean Penny Postage move-ment, he addressed one hundred and fifty public meetings on the subject in England, Scotland, and Ireland, and travelled over nearly the whole of the United States to stir up interest and action in the reform. In 1854 he again returned to America, and laboured for six years to bring the government and people to adopt "Compensated Emancipation" as the safest, cheapest, and most equitable way of extinguishing slavery in the United States. He visited nearly every considerable town in the Free States, and urged at public meetings this mode of solving the great difficulty. He proposed that all the public lands in the Union should be appropriated to the compensation of the slave-holding States for the emancipation of their slaves, and endeavoured to show that a sufficient fund might be obtained from the lands to pay the whole expense of this great act of justice and freedom. A National Com-pensated Emancipation Society was formed to operate upon the mind of the nation in behalf of the plan, and considerable interest and some action had been gained

in Congress, when Old John Brown's descent into
Virginia intercepted all peaceful modes of settlement,
and precipitated that terrible arbitrament which extinguished slavery at a cost to both North and South ten
times greater, counted in money alone, than the amount
involved in peaceful compensated emancipation.

In connexion with these various movements, the
author necessarily travelled and laboured in different
countries, and edited several periodicals in England and
America. "The Christian Citizen" was commenced in
1844 and continued to 1851. "The Bond of Brotherhood" was started in England in 1846 and continued
till 1868. "The Citizen of the World" was published
for two years in Philadelphia, from 1855 to 1856
inclusively. "The North and South" in 1858 and
1859, in New Britain, Connecticut, devoted especially
to compensated emancipation. All the articles in
the "Sparks from the Anvil," "Voice from the
Forge," and "Peace Papers for the People," were
taken from "The Christian Citizen" and "The Bond
of Brotherhood," and were written between 1844 and
1850. All the contents of the present volume have
been taken from the aforenamed periodicals between

1850 and 1855 ; and from the circumstances alluded to they are literally " Thoughts and Notes at Home and Abroad." Should they be favourably received, the volume will probably be followed by another of similar character, filled with selections of later date. Although many of the papers here presented relate to movements and occurrences of special interest ten or twelve years ago, the author hopes that they contain sentiments, principles, and views which may be regarded as worth preserving in this form by the new readers they may obtain. To them especially he has addressed these observations in regard to his own life and labours, that they might better understand the allusions to circumstances not explained in the articles referring to them in the body of the book. It is for such readers, mostly of another generation, that he has given these facts of his personal experience.

Birmingham, October 10, 1868.

CONTENTS.

Contents.

THOUGHTS AND NOTES

AT

HOME AND ABROAD.

—o—

THE CENTURY CLOCK.

EIGHTEEN hundred and fifty! Then it is noon on the dial-plate of the nineteenth century. And have we reached such a high semi-centenary stand-point of time? Seventeen hundred and fifty—eighteen hundred—eighteen hundred and fifty. What eventful periods have been tolled off to humanity by these bells of time! What epochs in the life of nations; what spaces of human progress; what vicissitudes of experience; what revolutions and renovations of human society have been included in these three periods! Turn to any middle-aged man, and he will tell you that his grandfather heard the clock strike seventeen hundred and fifty. And that grandfather was a sensible man, and owned and tilled, it may be, the farm his grandson owns

and tills; and perhaps there was as much resemblance
in form and feature between him and his own son as
between the latter and his son.   In fact, no essential
or striking difference may have existed between these
three links of individual life.   If that grandson lives
and moves and thinks in this age of railways and
electric telegraphs, and has mastered ideas unknown
to his predecessors, his experience is rather a quiet
inheritance than an acquisition which has cost him
effort.   No great vicissitudes, revolutions, struggles, or
transformations may have changed their course or condition.   Their family line holds the even tenor of its
way on the tide of time.   But turn to the life of nations,
and what vast changes have marked their experience
during three periods which can be spanned by the united
memories of two individuals !

When the clock struck seventeen hundred and fifty,
there were about 3,000,000 of the Anglo-Saxon race
scattered sparsely, in little settlements, from the mouth of
the Mississippi to the mouth of the St. Lawrence.
What an epoch in the history of Christendom was
included in the next fifty years !   What long and sangui-
nary struggles convulsed Europe during this period !
And all, perhaps, originating in circumtances connected
with the settlement and development of the New World.
It was, virtually, an unbroken age of war and rumours
of war, and revolutions which shook down thrones and
dynasties.   From the Cossack on the Don to the painted

Indian on the Ohio, all peoples, tribes, and tongues seem to have taken part in these bloody conflicts. There were no railways nor electric telegraphs, nor any quick faculties of communication between peoples and countries in those dark years of mutual alienation and jealousy. Christian philanthropy confined its stinted charities at home, or, if it ventured abroad, it found no rest for the sole of its foot on the wild deluge of violence that covered the earth.

Then the clock struck eighteen hundred; and heedless of the great lessons of the past, the nations of Christendom lighted the new century into the world with the torch of war, and baptised its first years in the blood of three millions of human beings slain in battle, and that, too, in the name of the Christian religion. And it was not until the nations had given all their power to the beast of brute force, and lay exhausted from loss of blood and treasure, that a still small voice arose, uttering the rebuke of the Gospel against all war, and men began to associate their efforts to banish it from the earth. Slowly, evangelized ideas and benevolent thoughts took hold of the mind of the age, and germinated into great enterprises of philanthropy. Slowly, humanising arts and sciences worked out their feats on time and space, and all the impediments to the social intercourse of different countries and communities. The iron horse began to thunder across islands and continents. The steam ship trod the waves and the strong

head-winds of the ocean beneath its feet, and walked
the seas—a thing of giant life.   The wires of the
electric telegraph thrilled with messages sent by bitted
lightning from metropolis to metropolis.   Nations approached each other.   Old animosities paled before the
genius of another age.   Commerce plied its ceaseless
shuttles across the ocean and the sea, and, in the silken
warp and woof of mutual interests, inwove peoples once
alienated by hereditary animosities.   And over and
above, and through all these agencies, permeated the
ideas of Christian faith and the light of the re-revealed
revelation, that " God hath made of one blood all
nations of men."   Swifter ran the iron horse, and with
longer reach the steam ship paced the ocean, and the
lightning flew on smaller errands, and great nations
fraternized, and peoples of different tongue met in
congress to organize peace and brotherhood within their
family circle.   And now the great clock of time has
struck eighteen hundred and fifty.   The men who
remember the century's birth, and the early and later
years of its history, may command such a retrospect as
never came within the reach of one human vision or
memory since the Christian era.   No men who have
lived upon the earth were ever permitted to contemplate
the past and future from such a Pisgah of observation
as they have now reached.   What a vista of momentous
events to humanity must fill that retrospect !   What
changes, what progress, what new conditions in the being

of nations and individuals have they not witnessed!
They remember the slaughter-day of Waterloo, and all
the bloody days in which the infancy of the young
century was cradled. They remember the awful mélée
in which all the nations of Christendom took a ruinous
part, and acted out such an enormous drama of violence
as the world had never witnessed. How natural to contrast that period with the last fifteen years! To contrast
the brute-force conquests of the one with the moral-
force conquests of the other; the garments rolled in
blood, and the shout of victory on the field of Waterloo,
with the garments of praise and the freedom-shouts of
800,000 slaves in the British islands on the morning
of their emancipation; the bridge of Lodi, with the
bridge with which steam has spanned the ocean and
connected two worlds—England and France, with all
their Titan-handed energies, grappling in deadly struggle
on the field of battle, with England and France walking
arm in arm as mediators and peacemakers between the
nations whom they taught the art of war; the Peace
Congress at Paris, with the Congress of Vienna; the
principles enunciated at the one, with those which monarchs decreed divine at the other; the spirit of fellowship
and brotherhood between the peoples now, with their
mutual jealousy and alienation in 1815.

Eighteen hundred and fifty! Blessed be the young
eyes that shall see its future through of fifty years.
Blessed be the ears that shall hear the clock strike the

century hour of nineteen hundred.   Blessed be those
who shall ascend that Pisgah's top of time and look
back over the pathway of humanity to this hour, and
contemplate its great progress-points, and the events
of happy augury and impulse which shall divide the
distance, like illuminated milestones, along the road.
And blessed be the eyes that shall look future-ward
from that sublime stand-point and see what God has
prepared for human vision within the horizon of that
distant day.   And many eyes now fixed upon these lines
will see that day, and contemplate its past and future;
and some of the grey-headed men and women of that
epoch may remember these words in connexion with its
anniversary.   For there are thousands of young minds,
on both sides of the Atlantic, who have learned to
sympathize with the spirit of the philanthropic movements of the present day.   The men who have borne
the brunt and burden of these movements may be
permitted to pass over a little way into the Canaan of
the next half century; but one by one they will disappear, and the ark of the cause be transferred to the
shoulders of those now in the morning of life.   Children
of to-day, fathers of the first men of Nineteen Hundred,
GOD and humanity expect that you will do your duty
and be true to your high trust and vocation.

—◦—◦—

AGAIN IN THE FATHERLAND.

ONCE more we are in this dear old fatherland—on this green garden-island of the world; and the fragrance of its shade-embowered homes is again as fresh as the sentiment of sweetbrier or anything that blooms and breathes out of hedge or meadow. Land of the Penny Post—it seems good to be here again, where all the birds sing, and the hedges are full of music, and the lark climbs the sunbeam with its warbling heart of joy—and fields of the greenest green are threaded with the foot-walks of a century's wear, and stiles of kindly ingress. Wonderful island! fatherland of sixty millions now, and, before a century and a half shall deepen the wrinkles in the brow of yonder church, half hidden in the trees, it shall be the fatherland of three hundred millions of Anglo-Saxons, peopling the islands of all the oceans, and all the distant regions of the world. What a fulcrum-point this for that moral lever that shall lift the race of men to its true position in the scale of being!

—◦—◦—

THE RAUHE HAUS AT HAMBURGH.

I N no city that I have visited in Europe is human kindness more extensively and minutely organized than in this commercial capital of Northern Europe. In the first place, you find hospitals fc· all ages and all conditions of bodily affliction; houses of correction, refuge, and rescue. Then the out-door benevolence is administered after the most perfect system of order and activity. This department of charity is managed chiefly by the ladies, and no nook of poverty or wretchedness escapes the vigilance and visitation of their lovingkindness. It would be impossible to do more than name all these institutions and operations of philanthropy in one letter, so I will occupy this with an account of one of the number, which seems to embody the spirit of all the rest in the most interesting and striking manifestation. This is the "Rauhe Haus," established in 1833. The literal meaning, as nearly as it can be given in English, of this appellation is, "The Rough House," or a house of refuge for the rudest, most hopeless little vagabonds of beggary and vice that can be found in the lowest lanes and sewers of poverty and sin. In this institution, these young beings, whose every day of life has been a year of wretchedness and crime, are brought under the action of two cardinal principles—the law of kindness, and the influence of family society. As an illustration of the power of these principles in transforming what would seem to be the very mistletoes of humanity into trees bearing the best fruits of virtue, this institution is yet unequalled, although several of the kind have recently sprung up in different countries. A cursory glance at its history will suffice to delineate the principal features of its character.

On the 1st of November, 1833, J. H. Wichern, an earnest man, whose heart is a living gospel of Christian love to his kind, took possession, with his family, of a small, one story, straw-roofed house, fronting on a narrow lane leading out of the village of Horn, about three miles from Hamburgh. This little building itself was a vagabond house, having been what would be called in America a "rum hole"—a resort for the lowest and noisiest kind of drinkers and smokers. About an acre of land, covered with sprawling bushes, ditches, hillocks, &c., formed, with the smutty cottage, the foundation of the new institution, which was to solve another great problem in the mysteries of humanity. No great palace or prison-looking building had been erected by the State for this experiment of benevolence. None was contemplated or desired. From the beginning to the end, it was to be a cottage establishment; and this one by the lane side, with its rum-seethed, tobacco-smoked walls, and roof of black mouldering straw, was all the heroic founder asked for the working out of his scheme of philanthropy. After the lapse of a week, spent in purifying this little cottage and preparing it for a home for the little unfortunate beings who were to be gathered to its hearth, three were brought in from their lairs on the frosty pavement or door-stones of the city. In the course of a few weeks, fourteen of these young vagabonds were introduced within the fold of that family circle, varying from five to eighteen years of age, yet all old in the experience of wretchedness and vice. Each had become a hardened veteran in some iniquitous practice or malicious disposition, and, as such, had been pronounced or regarded as incorrigible. Nearly all of them had been left and trained to beggary, lying, stealing, and to every vicious habit. Some had the organ or disposition of destructiveness developed to such a frenzy, that the first thought of their life seemed to be the mutilation of every thing they could reach; others had acquired a ferocious force and obduracy of self-will. One of these adepts in crime had been convicted by the police of ninety-three thefts, and yet he was only in his twelfth year. They had been treated or regarded as a species of human vermin, baffling the power of the authorities to suppress. They had slept under carts, in door-ways, herding with swine and cattle by night, when the begging or thieving hours were past. Such were the boys that found themselves looking at each other in wonder and surprise the first evening they gathered around the hearthstone of that cottage home. There was no illusion about this sudden transformation of their experience. There was that bland, benevolent man in their midst, with his kind eyes and voice, looking and speaking to them as a father to his children. And there was his mother with the law of kindness on her lips, in her looks, in every act and word; and he called her mother, and they called her mother, and the first evening of their common life she became the mother of their love and veneration; and they—ragged, forsaken, hopeless castaways, conceived in sin and shapen in iniquity, became the children of her affection. As far as the east from the west, was their past life to be separated from their future—to be cut off and forgotten. And this cottage, away from the city and its haunts, with its bright fire by night, and the little beds under the roof, with its great Bible and little psalm-books, was to be their home. And the great chesnut tree that thrust out its arms over it, and all the little trees and the ditches, hillocks, and bushes of that acre were their own. Some hymns and sweet-spirited ballads were sung after the frugal supper, and then the mother of the circle told them some nice stories with her kind voice; and the father, with his kind eyes, asked their advice about some little plans he had in his mind for improving their farm. The feeling of home came warming into their hearts like the emotions of a new existence as he spoke to them, with his kind voice and eyes, of our house, of our trees, of our cabbages, turnips, potatoes, pigs, and geese and ducks, which we will grow for our comfort.

That night the boys went up to their beds under the roof, wondering if all this would be real in the morning, or if they should wake up on the frosty door-stones of the city, or under the carts, and find it all a dream that they had experienced in the few hours of that new life. The morning came, and, with its first ray of light, the kind eye and voice of the family father; and they gathered around the breakfast table, and then for a little while around the fire, and a hymn was sung; and then they all went out together to commence the work they had agreed on in the council of the fire-side the night before. It had been unanimously voted that a sprawling wall of earth, half surrounding their garden, should come down first; and at it they went in earnest, with such tools as they had. And no small job was this for fourteen boys from five to eighteen years of age, for it was 500 feet in length, and six in height and breadth. That first day's work was a triumph to them, and when they grouped around the fire at night, the ambition of new ideas came into their hearts. There were tools wanted for rooting out the briars and bushes, and there were boys of the circle that would undertake to make them. They went so far as to speak of making a tool-house; nay, even a shop where they would work in stormy weather. The oldest boys were sure they could build it alone. At the end of the first week they had made a year's progress in this new life and its hopes and expectations. The earth mound gradually disappeared, and the faith that they could do something, be something, and own something grew daily within them; and they sung cheery songs at their work; for almost every evening they practised on some ballad, under the instruction of the mother of the circle. "So eager did they become to accomplish this undertaking," says the first report of this institution, "that they frequently worked by lantern-light in the evening, rooting up bushes and trees, in spite of snow and rain." The winter days and nights came, and when they could not prosecute their out-door work, their united genius contrived employment within. The family-mother taught them to knit and sew, and other arts of domestic industry; and in the long winter evenings, after recreating for an hour in reading, writing, or ciphering, they gathered into a circle on the floor—a little band of cross-legged tailors—and plied their needles of every size on thick, coarse stockings, frocks, trousers, &c., and some the awl on shoes, half wood and half leather, for the future inmates of their home, who might be brought in from such places as they themselves once inhabited. This was a work and a thought that brought kind feelings into their hearts, and many a one of the group wondered how such and such a boy, who used to cuddle down with him of a frosty night on a door-stone in the city, would feel in the frock or trousers he had under way. This was their singing time; and just in proportion as they loved to work they loved to sing, and they did both on these occasions with the happiest zest. They were taught the most lively and joyful tunes first, and these took the precedence in their music and labour concerts of the winter evenings. Then came the spring with its music and beauty and birds and bees, and all things green and gladsome; and with it came to the boy-family of the Rauhe Haus a new life of labour, hope, expectation, and plans. During the winter their number had increased, and their beds were too thick under the roof, and their ideas had taken a house-building turn during the long evenings, and some of the older boys had tried their hands at the model of a cottage, and all had come to the faith that they could build a house large enough to live in. The plan was drawn out first on the floor with chalk, then with ink on paper, and they longed for the winter to be gone with its frost and ice, that they might break ground with their spades and picks for the cellar. As soon as the snow-banks disappeared they fell to with an ambition which took hold of the youngest of them, to build a house for themselves all alone. As soon as daylight came, and as long as it lasted, they were seen and heard singing at their labour. "On the 11th of March," says the first report, "the foundation of this, the first kinderhaus (children's house) was laid, with prayer and singing, in the presence of several friends of the institution, favoured with the most beautiful weather. All the earth-work on this 'Swiss-house,' as it was named, had been performed by the boys. They dug the cellar, carted the bricks, prepared the mortar, and now the walls began to rise, and their joy to rise. Every boy, great or small, held on to the work, longer and later, until, on the 16th of April, the whole company, with a jubilee of song, hung a wreath of triumph on the gable of the house. A few more busy days, and the building was completed, and ready for the reception of the first colony from the old Rauhe Haus. It was hung from top to bottom with evergreens and wreaths of flowers; and on the 20th of July," says the report, "on a bright Sabbath morning, it was dedicated, in the presence of several hundred friends, to the good Shepherd, through whose love and help already twenty-seven boys had taken up their residence therein."

This event opened a new chapter in the social economy and moral character of the institution. The affections, hopes, sympathies, and enjoyments of these boys all clustered around this family life. They had lived, laboured, slept, eaten, and sung together for many months; they had built them a home together, and now they took possession of it with joy and exultation. An earnest, young disciple of the law of love, who had come from a distance to discipline his heart and life to a régime of kindness, and who had lived in their midst as an elder brother, accompanied them to their new dwelling, to live with them still as a fatherly brother and companion in labour, study, play, and in all their enjoyments. Another young man, of the same spirit, entered the old hive or Rauhe Haus, where a new family of little vagabonds from different parts of the country began to form. In the course of time, this also colonized in the same way as the first, and took up their abode in a cottage-home, built mostly by their own hands, taught and assisted by the elder family of the "Swiss-house."

Thus has this most interesting institution expanded gradually into a little cottage village of boy-families, each having their own separate house and home, and their fatherly brother, a young man of twenty or twenty-five years of age. Feeling at a loss how to spend "Thanksgiving Day" properly in a foreign land, I determined to spend it in visiting this establishment. So I walked out to it from Hamburg, a distance of about three miles, and was most kindly received by one of the young men of the institution. He took me through all the workshops and dwelling-houses, their little chapel, the wash and drying house, their printing office, bakehouse, &c. It was truly a beautiful spectacle, to see these young beings, once so hopeless, wretched, and vicious, now sitting clothed in a better mind, so full of hope and gladness and gratitude. There they were, parcelled into little groups, with one of "the *brethren*" in the centre of each, busy at every species of utilitarian handicraft. They are all shoemakers, tailors, blacksmith, carpenters, &c., by turns. For a certain length of time, a troop of

them, with a "brother" at their head, may be found
mounted on shaving-horses, and showing themselves a
brave little band of coopers; then they may be seen
sitting cross-legged in a ring on a large platform, plying
their needles to the same tunes on garments for the
whole community, and for future comers. For it is the
motive of this economy, not only to teach them all
kinds of handicraft, but also to discipline their minds
to the habit of working for each other.

There are now about seventy boys and twenty-five
girls in this establishment, who constitute four boy-
families and two girl-families, both sexes varying in age
from eight to sixteen years. There are from thirty-six
to forty "brothers," and eight "candidates," or theo-
logical students, preparing for the ministry, by taking
lessons in the law of love, as here put in force. Thus,
not only these young creatures are rescued from ruin,
and transformed to a new life, but scores of earnest
young men are trained for superintendents and founders
of similar institutions in other countries.

The moral and religious development of these children
would form a history by itself, which would be deeply
interesting to every benevolent mind. First among the
influences that opened their hearts to a Christian culture,
was that of music. "Especially at first," says the report,
"it happened almost daily that some of the larger as
well as the smallest boys broke forth in sobs, and wept
aloud during the singing in our morning devotions; and

C

on one occasion the whole were so deeply affected as to be obliged to give it up. 'We cannot hold out singing,' they were accustomed to say, 'without thinking of what we have been.' On one occasion, when they were by no means learning and practising church melodies (to which a special hour on the Sabbath was allotted), one of the boys stood as if out of his mind. On my speaking to him, he said, 'During singing I forget everything here, and think only of my former life.' On another occasion, two brothers fell into each other's arms, and were so affected that I was obliged to send them into the garden; for they had thought of their unfortunate mother while engaged in singing. Especially with the spring increased their joy in this exercise. In the evening, after their work was done, they gathered of their own accord around a tree, or laid down on the grass, or walked arm-in-arm, a whole hour long, in the garden, and sung their beautiful songs; or they climbed at vesper time, with their bread, to the highest branches of the beautiful chesnut and lime trees that overshadowed the *Rauhe Haus*, and mingled their songs with those of the feathered songsters."

I have been able to give but a cursory glance at the history and principal features of this interesting institution of benevolence; but I hope enough has been said to demonstrate the fact, that no human being can sink below the reach and rescue of human kindness, when breathing with the love of GOD and man.

—◦—◦—

CHRISTMAS AT THE RAUHE HAUS.

KNOWING what a day of gladness, and greetings, and gifts of loving remembrance Christmas was, in all home-circles, in hospitals, in the richest houses of the rich, and in the poorest houses of the poor, I resolved to see its working and enjoyment at this interesting institution. So, at about twelve o'clock, I wended my way thither. It is situated in the village of Horn, about three miles from Hamburgh; and, on turning off from the main road into the narrow lane which led to it, I found that scores of people from the city were proceeding thither—some on foot, others in carriages, to witness the celebration of the anniversary by the inmates of the establishment. The great garden, full of cottages, seemed to smile with the gladness which throbbed in the hearts and shone from the faces of the hundred happy children which it embosomed. The trees which they had planted, thicket thick, around their little houses, seemed to lean to each other lovingly, and to wish each other a " merry Christmas;" and the ducks and geese in the lakelet, and the merry chickens that nestled or sported in the sunny places in the garden, appeared to know and share the day's experience. The visitors or spectators of the scene began to accumulate into a crowd about the door of the little chapel; and many a richly-appointed carriage drove up and set down parties of distinguished rank from Hamburgh, who came to see the happiness of children recently rescued from its lowest scenes of vice and poverty, and renovated to a new existence. In a few minutes the family church of this family of cottages was completely filled, with the exception of a small space at the desk-end of it, which was reserved for the boy and girl families, and their "Father" and elder "Brethren." At the foot of the desk was planted a Christmas-tree, which reached to the ceiling overhead, with every branch holding in its hand a taper light. A little way in front of this, a semicircular table was arranged, covered with white linen, and extending, in its diameter, nearly from wall to wall. On the outer or convex side was placed a row of chairs for about thirty persons, which seemed to be reserved, as I imagined, for special guests or dignitaries from the city—perhaps the principal patrons of the institution; for all the other seats were mere hard benches without backs, and these were already occupied and crowded by persons of all ages and conditions. In a few moments, however, I felt reproved for appropriating in my imagination these thirty reserved chairs of honour after the common standard of estimation. There was a movement at the door of unusual interest. Those standing close by it made way deferentially for a party, the special guests of the occasion, who were to go up higher than they, to the highest places at the feast. They came—the poorest of the poor, the lamest of the lame, the blindest of the blind, the oldest of the aged. From the lowest habitations of poverty, in the neighbouring villages, they came at the invitation of these reformed little vagabonds, whose hearts were softened to the kindest issues by souvenirs of "the hole of the pit," of that wretchedness and perdition from which they had been rescued by the hand of Christian love. And of this love and charity having freely received, grace for grace, their young hearts and hands were going to give back freely to these poor and decrepit people, gifts of their gratitude to GOD and man for their own salvation. An old woman, of ninety-six years, led the way, and was seated in the chair of honour at the centre of the table, and those on each side of her were filled by pauper guests from the hovels, hedges, and highways of the neighbourhood. The next minute, the quick, short tread of a multitude of young feet, and mingling with the murmur of young voices, was heard without, and the father of the institution entered at the head of its children-families, numbering about 100 boys and girls, from five to eighteen years of age, and accompanied by the band of "Brothers" who live with them, as the heads and companions of their home and labour circles. For a few minutes the house was filled with the lively clatter of their wooden-soled brogans, as they crowded into the small space between the guest table and the wall, and rounded up into a hill of happy

faces, scores of which peered out floridly, with eyes of
large expectation, from the branches of the Christmas-
tree. The father-superintendent, a man about forty-five
years of age, with long apostolic locks of silver grey, and
eyes and voice full of heaven, and the sympathies and
affections of the heart into which it descends and dwells
with its music, and love, and river of life, and all its New
Jerusalem of joy, and who had brought all these to
bear upon the rescue and renovation of these children of
poverty and sin—stood before us. The special guests
of this feast were the first objects of his observation;
and he stepped forward, and with his face beaming with
the light of loving-kindness, and voice modulated to its
sweetest accents, he gave his hand to each of the circle
in succession; not merely with a passing inquiry or
greeting of good-will, but with a short, tender address of
sympathy, cheer, and exhortation. The windows were
now darkened, and the tapers, with which the Christmas-
tree blossomed, were lighted, and looked a very star-tree,
bringing out in bold relief the light-haired heads and
sunny faces that nestled under its green branches, all the
greener for the light-blossoms they bore. The religious
exercises were opened by a Christmas anthem by the
children, who made such heart-music of it as I never
heard before. What a choir that! It seemed a melody
almost divine. Every voice and eye of them all sang
with a melting power of sentiment, which it was a privilege to see as well as hear; for ás their voices swelled

up into the sublimest unison of the anthem, their ruddy
faces softened and shone with the ecstasy of the music
in their hearts. This was followed by a prayer addressed
to the Throne of Grace by the father of the children-
families, with his eyes open, fixed, and wide, and seeming
to look clear into heaven and see the blessing he asked
upon us all. Another anthem followed this, and then a
glowing, eloquent address from the superintendent, which
lasted about an hour. To those who have read the
gospel sermon of his life it would be unnecessary to say
how such a man must preach, so I will not undertake
to describe it.

At the conclusion of this address another hymn was
sung, and then came the consummation of this interesting
scene. The superintendent, with the liveliest emotions
of pleasure, in which the whole congregation participated, described graphically the Christmas gifts which
the children had presented him and his wife, and
children by blood, on the previous evening; the embel-
lishments of the room, the devices of their genius, the
fairy chapel, and castles of moss and evergreen, cottages
of bread, and pyramids of cake and confectionery, &c.,
all of their own handiwork. And now they had called
in these poor guests before them, from the abodes of
poverty in the surrounding villages, to present them gifts
of their good-will and sympathy. He then called upon
the representatives of the different boy-families to bring
forward the presents they had prepared for the occasion.

The family of the "*Swiss-house*," the eldest daughter of the mother-house, was first invited to bring their Christmas offerings. Each of these families, it will be recollected, consists of sixteen or eighteen boys, every one of whom had a gift for one of the pauper guests on the outside of the table. But as they could not all come forward to it, four of their number were delegated to present their offerings. And they ranged themselves beside the father, with their arms filled to their utmost embrace with everything good and comfortable to the poor, in all weathers—with coarse stockings, wooden-soled shoes, thick and warm articles of clothing, and with huge loaves of brown bread, &c., all of their own hands' making. The representatives of the "*Bee-hive*" family were next called, and they came forward with their arms full of similar gifts; and were followed by those of the other houses. In like manner the two girl-families brought theirs, and stood with them in their arms, over against the poor old women who were to receive them. Then they all broke forth spontaneously in a hymn, which breathed in music the spirit with which they were about to lay these humble offerings of their hearts before the subjects of their benevolence. In the midst of the hymn they paused, as if a new thought had struck them all. The father stepped forward to the little desk, and took up the Bible, as if it had been the ark of the covenant, and read those verses in the 25th chapter of Matthew which describe the scene when the SON of Man shall come in His glory, and all nations be gathered before Him, and "The king shall say unto them on his right hand, Come ye blessed of my FATHER, inherit the kingdom prepared for you from the foundation of the world; for I was an hungred, and ye gave me meat; I was thirsty, and ye gave me drink; I was a stranger, and ye took me in; naked, and ye clothed me; I was sick, and ye visited me; I was in prison, and ye came unto me:" and when, in answer to the question of surprise—when and how they had ever administered unto Him after this manner—He shall answer, "Verily, I say unto you, Inasmuch as ye have done it unto one of the least of these my brethren, ye have done it unto me." He closed the book and said, that on the eve which they were commemorating, our heavenly FATHER had presented a Christmas gift to mankind, which exhausted the wealth of the universe. In JESUS CHRIST He had given us all things, both the riches, and fulness, and glory of the Godhead. We could not give back anything to Him, personally, for all that we had and were was His, and came from Him. But still, He had surrounded us with the objects of His loving-kindness, through whom He would accept the smallest gifts, deeds, and thoughts of sympathy and good-will, as done unto Himself. "Inasmuch as ye have done it unto the least of these my brethren," said he, turning the palms of his hands outward toward the poor creatures before him, who were weeping at his words, "ye have done it unto

me." Through these, the least of His little ones, these
children may each present a Christmas gift to the SAVIOUR
of the world, who, in his manger-cradle, brought life and
immortality in His baby hand, and gave the greatest gift
to all mankind that GOD could give and man receive.
It was infinitely striking, and the whole company seemed
as if listening to a new gospel. I never before heard
or saw those passages applied by such illustration.
Then the hymn was resumed, and the voices of the
happy little multitude careered from unison to unison
in a rhapsody of harmony, until those who had joined
with them from the congregation gradually fell off, as if
to listen to the melting melody of those young and
happy hearts. No pen that I can wield could describe
that spectacle. It would require the pencil of a master-
hand to have portrayed its leading features. Perhaps
the imagination of our young friends may draw a picture
of the scene. Can you not, then, see, in the foreground,
the father of the children-families, a tall man, with his
kind eyes and long hair of silver grey, and a voice
modulated to the sweetest accents of benevolence, with
his heart full to overflowing with gladness and gratitude
to God, for the working of His grace to such a surprising
regeneration of the natures of the young beings that
clustered around him ? Then see those sixteen boys
and eight girls standing in the first rank, on each side
of him, with their arms full of Christmas gifts to the
poor old men and women before them, with their heads

inclined a little to one side, and with their eyes turned upward in fixed ecstasy, as if listening to music made in heaven, instead of their own. See that little boy, a dozen summers, with white hair and florid cheeks, with a loaf of bread in his arms, half as large as himself, and a dozen pairs of clog shoes, of his own make, singing with all the rapture of his heart's gladness. Can you not make a visible picture of it?

While the hymn was pealing upward on the swelling tide of all these voices, a movement of the eye from the father toward the four representatives of the Swiss-house family, gave them the sign, and they stepped forward, without dropping a note, and laid the gifts of "their house" on the table, before three or four of the decrepit old men, and then fell back into the line, singing all the while with increased enthusiasm. Then the representatives of the Bee-hive family stepped forward and laid its Christmas offering on the table, and were succeeded by the delegates of the other families in their turn. The table was piled two feet high with these gifts, but the hillock of them built up before the old woman of ninety-six, almost hid her from the sight of the givers. I will not add another word to the description. I believe our young friends can see, in imagination, the spectacle presented at this moment of consummation; and I would leave uppermost in their mind this aspect of a "Christmas at the *Rauhe Haus.*"

—◦—◦—

CHRISTMAS IN GERMANY.

CHRISTMAS in Germany is, indeed, an institution full of the beauty of loving-kindness and human brotherhood. In the first phase of its sympathies and susceptibilities, it would almost seem not only the celebration but the reproduction of the event which it commemorates; and that, too, with more than its original premonitions and anticipations, especially to all the children of the country, rich or poor. For weeks the heavens of their affections and hopes seem full of angels announcing the approach and advent of this day of joy and gladness. For weeks, their hearts and eyes are warm and wide with its hopes and expectations. As the interesting anniversary approaches, these are animated to new vivacity by the music of midnight anthems, and the sight of mid-day manifestations of good-will, which hail its advent. I had heard much of the festivities and felicities of Christmas in Germany; but my liveliest conceptions of them were infinitely surpassed by the reality which I witnessed in Hamburgh. For ten or twelve days before the anniversary, the brightening dawn of a happy event seemed to be heard, felt, and seen by the whole population. Their very business caught the glow of its morning light, and appeared to put on a gladsome

countenance. Heaven and home seemed to gravitate
into conjunction, by mutual and equal attraction; but
home was evidently the nearest and brightest orb of joy;
and all heavenward thoughts, and hopes, and aspirations
ascended to their goal through home, and the sanctities
of its affections. As the day approached, the bands of
singers and players on all kinds of musical instruments
increased in number; and from almost every other corner
of the streets, arose at midnight the great German
anthem, "*Nun danket alle Gott!*" The palpitating hearts
of all the children of the city were lulled to rest on their
hopes by the music of this sacred song. And in the
morning, as they trooped to school in bands, each with
his knapsack of books at his back, they found the great
streets and squares lined, thicket dense, with the Christ-
mas-trees which, on the great evening of their year's
expectations, were to be set up in all the homes of
Hamburgh, and illuminated with wax lights of every hue,
and hung with gifts of parental affection, which made the
eyes of their imagination glisten with joy. Had the fir
trees thus planted along the most public thoroughfares
and promenades of the city, been as high as the houses,
it would have appeared like a city built in a forest; for
there must have been at least two of these Christmas-
trees to every dwelling. The country people, who brought
in these little trees for the occasion, generally remained
by them all night long. At all hours of the day,
groups of children might be seen looking wistfully at

the young firs, with eyes expanding with their expectations, and seeming to ask, "I wonder which papa will
chose for us?" Every dealer had a little grove of
them; and for days before the great one of the anniversary, he busied himself in fitting bottoms or stands
to them, all in readiness to be mounted on the family
table, and to be illuminated and hung with gifts. Then
men and women were seen bearing them, thus prepared,
on their shoulders in different directions. The city grew
brighter and brighter by night, and every shop and
warehouse competed with its neighbour in the attraction
of its show-windows. The master-pieces of all fabrics,
and of every species of handicraft, art, and genius, were
put up in artistic witchery, for the multitude without to
gaze at, which they did by groups that blocked up the
side-walk, and sometimes extended far into the street.
Everybody, old or young, rich or poor, expected to give
and receive a Christmas gift; and the whole city seemed
to become a great bazaar for the exhibition and sale of
these tokens of mutual remembrance and good-will. The
carol bands sang later and louder by night; the windows
grew brighter with variegated illuminations; Christmas
trees were borne in every direction. The long-expected
evening came: it was very quiet; few people comparatively were seen in the streets; everybody was at home,
that had one, or was distantly related to one; and every
home circle in Hamburgh was grouped around a Christmas tree, which blossomed with souvenirs of home.

affections. In the lowliest dwellings of the poor, little
gifts bore testimony to these affections; and the youngest
and sickliest orphan in the hospital was bolstered up in
bed, and fondled in its shrivelled hands a doll, or some
token of remembrance from an unknown friend. No
one was to be forgotten in this dispensation of good-will.
The waiting-men and maidens at the hotels looked to
the guests for some mark of benevolent interest in their
welfare. Every individual, however lonely, wretched, or
forlorn, was to be brought within the pale and influence
of a home circle by some relation or other. Such circles
are formed merely for the occasion, when they are not
permanent. I was informed that married people who
have no children, and unmarried adults, frequently meet
together at the house of one of their number, on this
anniversary, and plant, illuminate, and embellish a Christmas-tree, and hang it with mutual gifts, and try to live
over again the memories of childhood connected with
this institution.

I was invited by a German family to witness the joy
of their circle on this occasion. I arrived a few minutes
before the time appointed for the opening of the scene.
The parents were busily engaged in the great room
dedicated to these offerings of affection, embellishing
the Christmas-tree, and arranging the gifts for their
children, in such a way as to surprise as well as delight
them with the manifestation. The children, on the
other hand, were on tiptoe with their plans for surprising

their parents with their little presents. It was a peculiar
feature of the charm of these gifts, that they were all
kept from each other's sight and knowledge. The
drawing of a windmill, or of a Swiss cottage in winter
which the youngest boy was trying to produce suddenly
before the parent eyes that doated on him, was the
unobserved work of moments which he had saved from
recreation for many preceding weeks. All was ready,
and the father gave the signal. The drawing-room door
was thrown open, and the fairy vista of the Christmas-
tree, with its green foliage full of variegated wax-lights,
illuminating the gifts arranged around it on the long
table, burst upon the young eyes that took in the bliss
of the sight at one glance. The whole family circle,
including grandparents, uncles, &c., grouped themselves
around the table, with the children in the middle, whose
hearts twittered with joy as they gazed upon the presents
that lay before them. Each had a gift appropriate to
his or her age. There were two of the band—two
sons just emerging into young manhood, who, in a few
months, were to leave the home of their youth, and to
set up for themselves the business of life in America.
It was evident that the presents to them had reference
to this pensive event in their experience. They included
articles that would be serviceable to them on the voyage
and in the New World. No direct allusion was made to
their departure; but it was easily to be seen, from the
tenderness of the affectionate wishes they exchanged

with their parents, that they all had the hour of separation in their hearts, and the thought that came with it, that this was the last time their family circle would all meet around the Christmas-tree.

—◦—◦—

THE SOCIAL PRINCIPLE.

WE hardly know where the social principle begins to work out its concentric circles of society; but we are inclined to believe that the first it forms is the one that centres itself to the family board or hearth. Perhaps, in the early life of the principle, a family circle of two parents and nine children, with the little unweaned one, made a world by itself for awhile; but another little world of the same size, by social attraction, or some other accident, soon appeared in sight; then another, and another, and, in process of time, a dozen of them got within the orbit of a little social system, called a neighbourhood. Then, in a few years, that neighbourhood grew into a village, then into a town. Well, at the distance of about ten miles or so, another family circle had grown into another town in like manner, and, before many years had elapsed, the third concentric circle of society had been formed, or a neighbourhood of towns, and which, in some countries, is now called a county, province, or duchy. The social principle worked on, and, after surmounting a little excess of centripetal attraction, or that feeling which centres an individual, family, or community to self, it worked out the fourth of its series of concentric circles—a neighbourhood of counties or provinces, commonly called a state, kingdom, or nation. This was a most laborious feat of the social principle, and cost it the busy application of many centuries of industry before it could make this last great circle work as harmoniously as the second in its series — the neighbourhood of families. And even now this great circle is not quite perfect; but it will, ere long, yield to the harmony of the inner ones. The social principle has acquired strength of attraction from every new circle it has added to its system, and, with that strength, it has been working on for years, night and day, day and night, with ten thousand agencies, great and small, visible and invisible, material and moral: it is working on day and night, night and day; across seas of blue and billowy waters, working; across the widest oceans ever ploughed by keel, working; under ground and above ground, and through tunneled mountains, working; on nerves of wire, thrilled with the lightning message of distant necessities, and of wants, social, commercial, and religious, that would charge the quickest wings of thought to bear their importunities across the ocean and the sea. On all these it is working night and day, day and night; working out the last sublime circle of its series—the Neighbourhood of Nations. It is pleasant, and the vision is full of promise, to trace this circumferent line which the social principle is now drawing around all the minor circles and harmonies of humanity. A neighbourhood of nations with all the affinities, kindly approximations, intercourse, copartnerships, intermarriages, and common necessities, which compact the society of a neighbourhood of families! Yes, it will come, and with it the better day will come. Daily the social principle adds to its centralizing agencies some new necessity of union, some strong penchant which makes great and multitudinous peoples lean and yearn towards the prime condition of that neighbourhood which is the first stage of Universal Brotherhood.

—◦—◦—

THE BROTHERHOOD OF NATIONS.

THE morning light of "the good time coming" is everywhere breaking upon the eyes of those who are looking and longing for its appearing. Everywhere new hearts and new hopes are gained to our cause. New agencies and tendencies are everywhere uniting to impel it forward. The great necessities and interests of the age combine to make peace the first want and predilection of nations. The fatherhood of GOD and the brotherhood of men are coming to be recognized by science and civilization, as well as by Christianity. This grand, central principle of divine revelation is taking effect upon the peoples of the world. The bristling barriers of nationality, which have hitherto divided and alienated them, are everywhere disappearing, and they are beginning to fraternize with each other across the boundaries which once made them enemies. The great transactions of nations, the mighty works of human skill and energy, are becoming international, not only in their benefits, but in their ownership and construction. Is it a canal that is proposed?—it is a channel for the ships of all nations across the Isthmus of Panama, to unite the Atlantic and Pacific Oceans, and shorten the passage to India by 6,000 miles. Is it a railway that is projected?—it is one 4,000 miles in length, across the Continent of North America, to open to the nations of Europe a north-west passage to China, of thirty days from London; or it is one to be constructed from Calais to Calcutta for their equal benefit. Is it an electric telegraph?—it is one to reach around the globe, crossing Behring Straits and the English Channel, and stringing on its nerve of wire all the capitals of the civilized world between London and Washington. Is it a grand display of the works of art and industry, for the encouragement of mechanical skill?—it is an exhibition opened, without the slightest distinction, to the artists and artisans of all nations, just as if they were all equal subjects of one and the same government, and equally entitled to its

patronage and support. Is it an act affecting navigation ?—it is to place all the ships that plough the ocean
upon the same footing, as if they were owned by one
and the same nation. Is it a proposition to cheapen and
extend the facilities of correspondence between individuals and communities ?—it is "to give the world an
ocean penny postage, to make home everywhere, and all
nations neighbours." These are the material manifestations of the idea of brotherhood which is permeating
the popular mind in different countries, and preparing
them for that condition promised to mankind in divine
revelation. They are, as it were, the mechanical efforts
of civilization to demonstrate, in physical forms of illustration, the truth, that "GOD hath made of one blood
all nations of men."

—⁌—⁌—

INTERNATIONAL SYMPATHIES.

TO one who watches with lively interest every indi-
cation of progress in the brotherhood of nations,
it must have been a token for good, which softens the
great affliction of the event, to witness the emotions of
profound sympathy manifested by different countries
towards England on the loss she sustained in the death
of Sir Robert Peel. Does it not prove that great
nations are susceptible of generous and fraternal sentiments of friendship for each other; that they, too, may

learn to rejoice in each other's joy, and mourn in each
other's sorrow; that, through the exercise and recipro-
cation of such feelings, they may contract attachments
as strong as those which can connect neighbour and
neighbour, friend and friend, strengthening down trom
generation to generation? Is there not something hopeful,
something to illustrate this fact, in the generous tribute
of sympathy proffered by the National Assembly of
France to England on the death of her illustrious statesman? In the next session of that body, after the news
of this event reached Paris, the president, M. Charles
Dupin, arose and said, " Gentlemen, at the moment when
a neighbouring people, our ally, deplores the loss which
it has just experienced in the person of one of its
statesmen, most worthy of esteem, I think it will be to
confer honour on the French tribune to express our
sympathetic regret on this occasion, and to manifest
our high esteem for the eminent orator who, during the
whole course of his long and glorious career, never
expressed any sentiments towards France but those of
kindly feeling and justice, and whose language was always
that of courtesy towards her government. (Loud approbation.) If the Assembly deigns to approve my words,
mention shall be made of the fact on the official minutes
of our sittings." (Unanimous marks of consent.)

—◦—◦—

WE.

WE is the beginning and end, the centre and circumference, the expression and expansion of all human societies, and of all the intelligent beings in the universe. An Almighty WE reigned in its eternal Godhead ere it breathed the first angel into its society, or spoke the first atom of matter into existence. Hence, till now, that pre-existing We has been working out the infinite concentric series of these mysterious social pluralities. There was a time when the first sun said We to its virgin satellite, when the first system of suns said We to all the worlds they lighted and led in their revolutions. The WE that bent their orbits proclaimed its everlasting plurality to the young earth on its first day's journey around the sun. "Let us make man in our own image," and We was the two eyes, and hands, and feet of that image, and therefore He created them male and female, that they might say *We* to each other, after the image of its prototype, for *I* could not live alone, even in Eden. Slowly, from the hour that the first pair of human beings recognized the plurality of their existence in the garden—We, the germ, centre, source, and circumference of all societies, human or angel, has been expanding towards its full and glorious consummation. There was a time when the two first families of the earth said We to each other; another two communities did the same; then villages, cities, provinces, clustered into the embrace of that first personal plurality, and said We with unanimous heart and voice, grouping their great interests, hope, faith, and deeds within a circle of patriotism, a national OUR. Humanity is in the last stage of this expansion, and the peoples of earth are gravitating into the commonwealth of this plurality. They are struggling to level the barriers of egotism, and to say We with each other; to expand their patriotism to the compass of the world, and make all their national interests, happiness, and progress OURS. Such is the destiny of humanity, prepared before the foundation of the world by that uncreated WE whom all that receive its divine manifestations call OUR FATHER in heaven.

—◦—◦—

THE HEROES OF HAMBURGH.

THE new Bourse of Hamburgh was built a few years before the great fire, in 1842, and escaped, almost by miracle, that fearful conflagration. A few heroic men, after the building had been given up to destruction, determined to peril their lives in a desperate effort to save it from the devouring element raging around them. The leader of this forlorn hope afterwards remarked that,

while all were fleeing from the edifice, the thought of
that man who, in ancient times, fired the costliest building in the world, in order to perpetuate his name even
in immortal infamy, darted through his mind; and he
paused on the door-stone, and asked himself, why
he should not do and dare as much to save Hamburgh's
beautiful Temple of Commerce. In a moment his resolution was formed; and four or five others accepted
his challenge to remain with him to save the building,
or perish in the attempt. They ascended to the roof,
with a hose attached to the fire-plug appropriated to the
Bourse, and, with hearts that quailed not at the most
terrible scene and danger that ever surrounded human
beings, they set to work. An ocean of flame roared and
rolled its red waves to the clouds, which seemed to ignite
and blaze over their heads. Billow after billow it bore
down upon them, melting, in one burning sea, whole
blocks and streets of houses around them. The ghastly
skeletons of churches fell with a groan and a crash at
their feet. The glowing, booming sea widened, and the
dark shore of the unconsumed city receded from them,
and the voices of its terrified inhabitants, as they slowly
retreated before the overwhelming element, grew more
and more like the confused noise of distant ocean-
breakers in a storm. But there the little band stood
upon that thick-walled building, pointing their hose at
every stone, at every corner and cornice. The water,
which was ankle-deep on the roof, became so hot as

almost to crisp their boots; but every one stood to his
post. Occasionally heaps of paper would take fire in the
different apartments from the heat of the floor, but were
soon extinguished by the patrols, who hastened from
room to room, with bucket in hand. A day and a night
they breasted the fiery tempest. The surrounding sea
of ruin began to blacken; the water on the roof and
floors to cool; the ashes and embers of a thousand
buildings to smoke with more humid vapours. They
waited yet a few hours for the deluge to subside, and
then one of their number opened a door, and dashed
into the hot, blinding waste toward the nearest shore of
the standing city. Through the burning wrecks he
threaded his way breathless, for he could not breathe;
now knee-deep in glowing ashes; now stooping under
overhanging crags of fire; now covering his face before
sudden simooms of scorching vapour; now springing
upon the site of streets barricaded with ruins, he at last
reached the Zoar, which had been saved from the awful
destruction, and brought back succour and rescue to
his heroic comrades in the Bourse.

—◦—◦—

TRADES AND THEIR TRANSFORMATIONS.

DURING our sojourn in Hamburgh, a little incident occurred, which seemed to indicate the approach of " the good time coming," when the sword shall not only be beaten into a ploughshare, but when its epauletted wearer shall take part in its honest service to mankind. A Swedish officer took up his quarters, for a few days, at the hotel in which we resided, and was presented with one of the German Olive-leaf pamphlets, which we caused to be distributed among all the guests of the establishment. The next day the officer came into our room, and expressed himself fully convinced of the truth and force of the arguments against war contained in the little brochure. " But," he asked, with serious tone and emphasis, "what shall we military officers do? This is our trade." He then fully and frankly described his condition. He had been educated for the army from his youth up, and he was the son of a general. He had graduated in the first university of Sweden, spoke five or six languages, was an accomplished scholar, and just in the prime of young manhood. Having studied for the army, and acquired the theory of the soldier's trade, he entered the Russian service, and went into the war with the Circassians, to learn the

practice of the profession, just as young American
surgeons go to France and other countries, to practise
in their hospitals, and under their professors of anatomy,
the art of setting broken bones, and of performing difficult and dangerous operations on the human body—
with the difference, that his trade was to break bones,
and gash human beings with wounds beyond the healing
of surgery. For four years he fleshed his blade upon
the Circassians, and acquired scientific skill in cleaving the
skull, transfixing the bosom, or lopping off the arm of
a fellow-being. Having thus perfected himself in the
art, he left the Russian service to practise his profession
wherever it should be most remunerative, and, perhaps,
honourable. His native country had nothing for him
to do in his line of business; so he repaired to Denmark,
as we understood, and offered his services to the Danes,
to fight the Schleswig-Holsteiners. But they had plenty
of officers, and declined his offer. He then proceeded
to Hamburgh, with the view of offering himself to the
Schleswig-Holsteiners to fight the Danes; being equally
ready and willing to draw his sword against one as the
other. But the war was drawing to a close, and could
not furnish him a job in his profession. " His occupation was gone;" and he seemed to open his eyes to its
uncertainty, and to the loss of time he had suffered
in learning the trade. He said he was ready to enter
upon any situation in civil life, which would afford him
support and employment of his talents. He was then

looking for such a place; and would prefer any honest business to his military profession. He admitted all its incongruities and immoralities, and wished himself well out of it. Taking up one of the Olive-leaves, he said he should like to translate them into Swedish, for circulation in that country. The idea was a pleasant one to our mind, and full of promise. It was turning the sword into a ploughshare, by an interesting process of transformation. It seemed to indicate what might come in coming days. It was one of the incidents of progress, of encouraging significance. If the first Olive-leaf that shall carry its message of peace to the people of Sweden, shall be put in their language by this officer whose other occupation was gone, it will make another incident of interest.

—o—o—

INTERNATIONAL SCHOOL OF COURTESY, 1851.

THE Great Exhibition will serve as a Normal School of Courtesy, in which nations will teach and be taught the deportment and proprieties of those delicate conditions of society, the relations of guests and hosts. We love to contemplate its influence in this direction. The nice perception of what pertains to these reciprocal relations, makes the charm of the most refined circles in private life. The spirit and grace with which they are

filled, are accepted as the first evidence of high cultivation. Look in upon a parlour-party of persons forming
such a circle of acquaintance. See what a bland spirit
of courtesy graces the bearing of guest to host, and of
guest to guest towards each other. What mutual deference and gentle efforts to put each other in the
highest seat! What palpable wish to commend hospitalities with the heartiest good-will on one side; to
appreciate and enjoy them on the other! What a
school for courtesy! But all the delicate responsibilities
which attach to these conditions of intercourse will
devolve upon the millions of different nations, who
will meet in London at the Great Exhibition. It will
virtually be a parlour-party of the people of Christendom.
They will put themselves into these nice relations with
each other on the magnificent occasion. To the usual
sentiment which attaches to the conditions of host and
guest, will be superadded the sense of those proprieties
which should illustrate and commend a nation's hospitality to strangers on one side, and its appreciation and
recognition on the other. The nations represented in
this mighty assembly will feel their honour staked upon
the deportment of their subjects who shall be present.
They will watch with solicitude that deportment, and
will experience a sense of humiliation, if it does not
become the courtesies of the occasion. So, on the other
hand, the whole British nation must comprehend these
responsibilities. They will devolve upon the whole

population of Great Britain, and concern the reputation of the entire nation. Every man must assume the disposition or character of a host; not the rich only, who may invite foreign visitors to his drawing-room, park, or gardens, but the day-labourer, the cabman, the waiter at the hotel, the railway porter, and every person who is called to render any service to one of the myriad guests of the nation.

What a school for courtesy; not the mere bowing, phrasy courtesy of conventional etiquette, but that which St. Paul describes, who had the best idea of a true gentleman of any man that ever lived; a courtesy that breathes a spirit of kindness; that does as well as bows; that goes with a foreign neighbour twain when asked to go a mile, to put him in the right way; that, instead of curling the lip at his language, interprets his words by the intuition of good-will and sympathy; that prefers him to the best place in the public walks; that says to him in expressions of kindness he can understand, without knowing a word of English, " Brother, I am glad to see you; what can I do to make you happy?" Great will be the part which the cabmen, porters, waiters, &c., will take in this magnificent demonstration. Great will be the responsibility devolving upon them, in discharging the first duties of the nation's hospitality. They will, we are sure, recollect that they are the first to act the host towards these foreign guests; the first to go out to meet them, with Britain's welcome; the last to pay them the parting hospitalities of the nation, to attend them a little on their way homeward. The first and last impressions will be received and retained from their deportment.

Come, now; what a school for Universal Brotherhood will this be to the labouring men of the metropolis and the nation! Fervently hope we that they will not only learn but teach the highest lessons in the law of kindness and courtesy.

—o—o—

THE CLOSING HOUR OF THE GREAT EXHIBITION OF 1851.

THE sun that told off to humanity the 11th of October, set upon the grand finale of the Great Exhibition. The day was exceedingly beautiful; as if given from heaven as its parting smile upon this mighty enterprise of human brotherhood. A vast multitude assembled in the Crystal Palace to take their last look at its world of wonders; not to examine them in detail, or by grand divisions, but to contemplate them as a magnificent whole, before their dissolution and dispersion among the lands that gave them being and beauty. The thousands present were generally of the middle class, including a great number of season ticket holders. The emotions that swayed the great congregation could easily be felt as well as seen. They had come to witness and

celebrate the consummation and conclusion of the most
illustrious event in human history for the last thousand
years. At a little before five p.m. they thickened in the
transept, and at the mouths of the avenues that debouched
into it, as if the moment of their expectations were close
at hand. The hands of the clock moved slowly to the
five hour mark. Then the great bells burst forth into
a thundering acclamation of triumph over the victory
achieved for humanity. Louder and louder they pealed,
until all the lofty arches thrilled and echoed with their
joyful clamour. Then they ceased for a few minutes;
when the vast multitude uncovered their heads, and the
National Anthem arose—solemn, grand, sublime. Ten
thousand voices, at least, mingled in this uprising flood
of joy and praise. The masses in the galleries looked
like so many mountains of life and emotion, one chanting
to the other in a mighty hymn of gladness. The scene
at this moment, and the sentiment and sympathy that
throbbed through the vast congregation, were indescribable. Like the scattered tribes of Israel that came up
to Jerusalem to worship in the Temple at Hezekiah's
invitation, even so these jubilant thousands seemed re-
luctant to leave the great Temple of Peace. Compact
they stood in the transept and main avenues, longing to
sing or shout for joy. Up rose cheer after cheer—the
spontaneous expression of an English assembly when
touched to a strong and common sympathy. Then singing
burst forth again, and a thousand voices struggled hard

E

to mingle in unison; but were wafted out of the stream
by the quick cross-currents of wondering gladness. Then
the bells tried it, and failed. The organs tried it, and
failed. Broken cheers arose from one part of the palpitating sea of human beings, and sacred psalms and
spiritual songs from another. The bells rung out their
cataract of clamour upon the murmuring flood of voices.
The organs said " Good night ! " to the bells; the bells
responded to the salutation. The very statuary seemed
moved to life and emotion by the quick, strong tides of
human feeling, and to play a part, of sublime expression,
in the grand finale. The great bay of human beings
began to thin through streetward rivulets. We stood on
the bridge that connected the two galleries in the transept, just over the main entrance, and watched the moving
multitude with such emotions as we never experienced
at the sight of a congregation of our fellow-beings.
Soon the avenues that debouched into the transept were
cleared nearly to their mouths, and barred across by the
police, to prevent any reflux of the retiring masses.
The bridge on which we stood was cleared several times
by the moral and mild persuasion of the men in leather-
topped hats, and filled again by a crowd eager to look
their last once more upon the thousands moving below.
At last this was barred also; and we descended to one
of the avenues, thinking to remain to the last man. But
we soon found this barricaded behind us, and policemen
stationed everywhere, " half hidden and half revealed,"

to expedite the egress with irresistible politeness. Thus we found ourself on the threshold of one of the entrances, with but a moment to turn back a look through the long, dim avenue, and bid farewell to a scene which never had had a parallel in the history of the world.

It was a beautiful autumnal evening, and as we crossed Hyde Park we turned around frequently to look at the Crystal Palace, which arose sublime in the golden twilight, serenely towering in glorious transfiguration, as if heaven embraced it with the halo of its smile, as THE TEMPLE OF UNIVERSAL BROTHERHOOD.

---o—o---

THE MOONLIGHT OF CHRISTIANITY.

THIS physical, outward world, with all its stereotyped ceremonies and phenomena, is incompetent to furnish a parallel to the working manifestations of that invisible world of spirit of which the being and attributes of GOD are the soul and centre. If such a parallel or parity could be found to things spiritual and eternal, in all nature's doings and developments, we might say, with close approximation to truth and propriety, that the civilization of the present day is the moonlight of Christianity. It is more than that; and it is the fault of the figure that the parity it portrays is so pale and defective. Modern civilization is more than the moonlight of Christianity, in several vital qualities. In light it is more; in warmth, a hundredfold more; in germinating faculty, a thousandfold more. In essence it is more in all these qualities; and in action, intensely progressing and everlasting. In light it is the same; but more in continuous and endless expansion. The first full moon that beamed upon Adam and Eve through the listening foliage of Eden, never borrowed from the sun an additional ray of light, for human eye or foot, from that hour to this; and never will, to its last rising. Christianity is the sun of civilization in a better, broader dispensation than this; and all the progress that mankind have made from the Egyptian darkness of barbarism has been by its light. There was a cold, fitful illumination that flushed the mosaic work and marble pillars of Grecian civilization in the day of Pericles, which, perhaps, this sun did not supply, even by indirect reflection. For even cold, inanimate substances of nature's realm contain and emit a luminous semblance, independent of sun or moon. When both are absent, and all the stars are veiled with clouds, the deep-drifted snow lightens, by several shades, the darkness of the night; and there is the same quality inherent in certain putrescent woods. And much more may the human intellect, in the phosphorescence of its mounting thoughts, produce a luminous glow without the light of divine revelation; and this may be called civilization; but for all that, it is like the light of snow, uncertain, dim, and cold, and treacherous as a guide.

Take it in its best illumination; in the brightest day of Pericles, and test its properties. What did man do by it then? Which way did he walk by it? What were the perceptions of moral purity and immortality, widening and deepening, which he grasped as he followed in its wake? Look at 1 is gods he invented and worshipped! Look at his gods! at Jupiter, Bacchus, Vulcan, or Venus! They were the sublimest embodiments of holiness, wisdom, and purity he could conceive! These were the divine ensamplers he set up; these the highest authorities in the universe that claimed his obedience and adoration! These he worshipped and imitated.

Conscience—like as the sunflower shut from the light, still upturns its yellow face to the path of the luminary which gives it its name—conscience, shut up from the light of divine revelation, in Greek, Helot, Parthian, bond, and barbarian, in like manner lifted up the blind petals of its innate sense to the existence and outgoings of some other GOD than these incongruous deities. Intellect, the most brilliant that ever shone in absence of revelation—intellect, that had harvested in all the fields of human science from the Flood, and treasured its arts, tastes, and talents in Athens, until it became the school of ethics, arts, and literature to the world— intellect made its greatest effort to satisfy this craving and clamour of conscience, and set up a marble image in honour of " The Unknown God;" and further than this it ventured not to go. Those who were exercised

with misgivings in reference to the character and administration of Jupiter and his subordinates, might ascribe
to this new deity whatever attributes they chose, and
worship him as they pleased.   That was all—the very
best—that heathen civilization could do for the human
conscience and its uneasy wants.

   This was plainly admitted to Paul by the Athenian
doctors and literati.   Then that bold apostle of JESUS
CHRIST stood up in the midst of Mars Hill, and Him
whom they had ignorantly worshipped declared he unto
them.   Over against the Mount Olympus of their gods,
he unveiled Mount Calvary.   Against the throne of
Jupiter Tonans, he ranged the red and rugged cross
of CHRIST, bleeding in meek humiliation for the salvation of the world.   Through His cleft side he pointed
them to a new world of holy immortality; in every drop
that followed the spear, to the seal of the fatherhood of
GOD and the brotherhood of men, of whatever country,
condition, or colour; in the celestial rays that haloed
His thorn-crowned brow, to the streams of divine life
flowing from His heart in heaven into the human soul,
transforming it to His likeness and filling it with His
spirit.   Strange doctrine, as well as new.   It was sheer
foolishness to the Greeks.   They rejected and scorned
it, as the vain babbling of an enthusiastic lunatic.   They
turned away with jeering incredulity to their schools.
They turned away to their gods with more vehement
homage.

But as they worshipped at their shrines, Mount Olympus began to dissolve. It slowly flowed down at the presence of the Godhead bleeding on Calvary. The throne of Jupiter trembled and fell, and all the secondary deities of his court fell like fictions to the ground. Few, scattered, and weak were the immediate disciples of Christianity at first, but there were myriads who followed it afar off, who found themselves indirectly affected by its teachings. From out of the false and shifting axioms of morality, it revealed a sublime and immutable standard, which showed the aberration and obliquity of the dogmas of heathen philosophy. Little by little, the proud and fastidious civilization of Greece and Rome, which had spurned Christianity and scourged and burnt its teachers, began to be affected by its influence. Gradually it absorbed into itself an element of that immortal life it sought to annihilate. Gradually the light it essayed to extinguish fell with wider revelation upon its own features, discovering their barbarity. One by one the bloody and cruel customs of idolatry fell with the fallen gods of paganism. Few and weak were still the followers of the persecuted faith, but, in realization of the promise, they were the light of the world, or the medium through which it shone outward—outward, farther and farther, even indirectly upon regions they had never seen.

Rome fell; but over the surges of barbarism that engulfed and buried it, shone out with steady ray the sun of Christianity. Anon, and for a season, its light seemed to be drowned in the flux and reflux of clouds breaking like black seas over the firmament. But behind them was still the sun, and before it they thinned, blanched, and vanished, revealing it shining in its brightness, reaching with its rays the remotest regions of Scandinavian paganism, and melting its icy superstitions. One by one the northern and nomadic tribes gave their idols to the moles and the bats; then rites, customs, ideas, and prejudices, that belonged to their worship. And, all this while, few, scattered, and weak were the real followers of CHRIST; but they were the light of the world; and it shone far, far beyond them, in constantly lengthening radiations. It created the civilization of the Teutonic and northern populations of Europe out of thick darkness; whilst it gradually transformed the old civilization of Greece and Rome more and more into its own likeness. The popular perception of the spirit and teaching of Christianity was faint and fitful; for the eyes born blind to its truths saw them at first, as once one saw men, " as trees walking." Hence some bloody and cruel usage belonging to dethroned idolatry was occasionally baptised even by teachers of Christianity into a rite and service of their holy religion. In the universal frenzy and enthusiasm of this delusion, all the nations of Christendom rushed into the Crusades, and thought to win heaven and life everlasting by wresting from infidel hands the sepulchre of a risen SAVIOUR and the site of His cross, on which He bled alike for all the families of mankind.

Few and scattered were the real followers of CHRIST, even at the moment when nearly all the kings and chieftains of Christendom were battling with the Saracens as the champions of the cross. But they were the light of the world, according to promise, and with longer-reaching rays; and they shone on from year to year, and from century to century. And as time rolled on, customs that had outlived many of their cognate iniquities, could not brook the light of a civilization penetrated and illumined by so many beams of Christianity. One by one they also loosed their tenacious hold on society, and fell under the feet of men. And now a day has come; and, comparing its revelations with those of other years, many are prone to call it the noontide of civilization. But this is a great mistake. The sun of Christianity is not shining at its noon yet, perhaps not by many centuries; and there will never be an afternoon of its power and light, while this above, that lights and centres our planetary system, shall hold its place in heaven. And until that hour, civilization will not have reached its meridian. Up to that hour, it will become more and more transfused with the light and surcharged with the elements of Christianity. Up to that hour, public customs, private habits, and universal ideas, which now bask seemingly in the sanction of the gospel, will, one by one, see by its shining that they are evil, and men will put them away with the things that have gone before.

Already civilization has become a kind of diffusive

conscience, covering, like an atmosphere, most of Christendom; and its moral sensibilities are becoming more and more lively and perceptive. Practices which half a century ago were deemed consistent even with professions of personal piety, are now condemned and rejected as immoral by those who make no such professions. Laws that were regarded as sanctioned by divine authority, and indispensable to the good order of society, are now remembered almost as relics of barbarism. Reproduce any of these customs and institutions at the present hour, and the atmosphere of public sentiment would thunder and lighten with indignation. Suppose some seemingly devout and praying Christian should go forth from the communion table to the shores of Africa, to trap or trade for human beings for the slave-market of Cuba or Brazil, as professing Christians have done almost within the remembrance of the living. In one of the provincial towns of England there stands the mound of the block, on which human heads were once struck off by the axe for the crime of stealing articles of as low value as thirteen-pence halfpenny; and the bye-law that ordered it stands in round, full type, in the records of the place, as if printed more recently than *Baxter's Saints' Rest.* Suppose that block should be re-mounted, and heads fall again for the same crime. Or imagine that law to be re-enacted, which stood unrepealed in the statutes forty years ago, by which two men, dissatisfied with the decision of the civil court, might refer their case to a personal combat at which the judge in his robes should be bound to preside in virtue of his office. Let any one of these public institutions or private practices be revived at the present day, and what a thrill of horror would run through the heart of the community!

Look at Intemperance, Slavery, and War, not in the moonlight of Christianity, but under its sunlight, shining through the civilization which it makes and raises, higher and higher, like an ever-mounting flood, in which the Law of Sinai and the Love of Calvary are blended and mirrored in one image of the divinity that is shaping the destinies of mankind. Look at these gigantic evils that have so long desolated the world. There they stand, like three huge, central citadels of sin, to which the minor systems of iniquity have fled, half-drowned, for refuge. There they stand, swaying, trembling, dissolving slowly before the beating surges of that shining flood. Will they fall, melt away, and disappear? Ask Isaiah, or any of the holy seers of old, to whom visions were given of the things that should come on the earth in the latter days of its existence. Will they melt away and disappear? Look at three icebergs, dragging their deep, frosty anchors southward from the frigid zone. See them slowly floating into the summer seas of the equator, beneath a tropical sun. Will they dissolve, and be seen no more? So will Intemperance, Slavery, and War. These vast sinbergs are floating abreast slowly into that

sea of public opinion lying close under the vertical sun
of Christianity. Abreast they swim; abreast they will
sink, if we read aright the signs of the times. Behold,
how equally the sea-waves of human opinion beat against
them! With what equal ray falls upon them the sun of
that civilization which borrowed no beam from the snow-
light of Grecian ethics in the palmiest day of their glory!
Which of them will fall first? Who can say? Who
need to know? Every love-drop distilled from Christian
charity into the sea that is mining and minishing their
foundations; every act, however small or secret; every
prayer, and hope, and wish that opens the individual
heart or the public conscience to a new perception of
the fatherhood of GOD and the brotherhood of men, and
to a deeper reverence for the duties and affections that
attach to those sacred relations, contributes to hasten
the downfall and dissolution of these gigantic evils.

THE NORMAL SCHOOLS OF PEACE AND WAR.

THE military system of Christendom has this year
assumed a new phase, which shows that it has
yielded, without a struggle, to the social tendencies of
this marvellous age. The commercial, manufacturing,
and industrial communities of the great nations are inter-

weaving their interests in a remarkable fashion. They are working into remarkable copartnership, conference, and comparison. They are working through, over, and under the barriers of jealous nationality, as if they were breaking gaol by candle-light. It is edifying to see them work, and witness the animus of their efforts. They seem to have caught hold of the material-interest aspect of the truth that "GOD hath made of one blood all nations of men." They seem to comprehend that an isolated community is a great *I* incarcerated in the narrow cell of its little self, and shut out from the companionship of the great *We* of mankind, and from all its endless affinities and interests. From this prison-house of I-hood, they are working into the great, green, glad world of We-hood, with millions of railway pickaxes, electric wires, and all the machinery and locomotion of steam. *We* is the watchword of all these great industrial populations. If "Westward Ho!" is the annual cry of half a million of emigrants to the New World, "*We*-ward Ho!" is the motto and the motion of the foremost nations of men. Never, since the first brick of Babel was laid, did the vast families of mankind say to each other with such unanimity as at present, "Come, let *us* build;" come, say *we* with us; come, co-work with *us;* come, take stock with *us* in this enterprise; come, let *us* build and own together this railway, this ship-canal; come, let *us* bore through this mountain, and bridge this sea, and lay a wire-path for the courier-lightning beneath the ocean. Science says this to labour, and labour to science; and all the arts and interests of peaceful industry are voiced with the same invitation to the permanent copartnership of peoples in the great works of the age.

Have you made any discovery in mechanical or agricultural science? Have you invented any machine to save or lighten the burdens of labour, to promote the comfort of man or beast? Bring it forth and put it into the common stock of public knowledge and utility. And thus we have come to an epoch of yearly World's Exhibitions of Arts and Industry, to which all the nations of Christendom contribute the master-pieces of their skill and handiwork. Go to London, to Dublin, to New York, to Paris. See what manner of inventions are here! See what generations of human genius, what a world of skill and labour, have been inspired with a good and brotherly sympathy with the wants of mankind in producing these things for the common weal! "Come, give, and take," is the motto written over the portal of every national department of science and industry. "You are welcome to all I can teach," says one to the other. "Have I anything here you can take home to your people, to make them more prosperous and comfortable; any idea or application of mechanical or agricultural science that you can adopt to advantage? If so, you are welcome to it." France shows to England the choicest specimens of her industrial artistry — all the infinite

modelry of chaste and elegant ideas wrought in drapery
and porcelain. England sets all the models of her
lodging-houses, washing and bathing-houses for the poor
before France. America brings out her reaping machines,
and says, " Try these instruments in your fields; they
are my humble contributions to the common weal of
labour." All the pacific tendencies of the times take
this direction—to internationalize the peoples of Christendom; to bring them into active and everlasting copartnership. International copyrights for literature and
patent rights for mechanical science, international railways, electric telegraphs, steam-packet companies, and
international exhibitions, have become the order of the
day.

All this is pleasant to witness, and more of it will be
seen from year to year, until all the nations of men shall
be fused into one peaceful brotherhood. But, as " When
the sons of GOD came to present themselves before the
LORD, Satan came also among them," so also the sons
and supporters of the war system seek to introduce
themselves, their ideas, tactics, and murderous machinery
into this international fellowship. They also, with their
irreconcilable antagonism, are yielding to the social tendencies of the times, and seem disposed to establish a
kind of *solidarité* of organization and interest. And they
are getting up exhibitions of the art of cutting each
other's throats ! At Chobham is reared the first Canvass
Palace of these destructive industries. Then follows the

grand display at Satory in France, then another in Prussia, and a fourth in Austria, all in one and the same summer! The machinery, both human and iron, displayed in these expositions of brute force, has doubtless been brought to great perfection. The modern reaping machines for mowing down the harvest of the battle-field, are here tested on stubble to the complete satisfaction of the skilled connoisseur of the military profession. Thousands and tens of thousands of admiring eyes witness with rapture the performance, and delicate women almost clap their white and jewelled hands for joy at the sight of the sounding charge. In common husbandry there are useful implements called clod-crushers, and in the husbandry of war there are analogous instruments, or the head-crushing hoofs of the cavalry; and how splendid is this mock operation on Chobham Moor, or the field of Satory! What outbursts of enthusiastic admiration does it call forth from the surrounding sea of spectators! How the thundering charge of the Horse Guards and the heavy dragoons over the broken infantry of the invisible enemy mingles in the dreams of a thousand young and ardent hearts, fluttering all the night long with the memories of the scene!

But the great and distinguishing incongruity of these military exhibitions is the strange and novel circumstance, that delegations of the generals of other nations are not only permitted but invited to be present, and to derive

an equal advantage from all these experiments and
lessons in the science of war. This is truly a new
development of the war system, and, though very odd
and unique, may be fraught with hopeful significance.
Who shall say to what it may tend, and in what it may
terminate ? Hitherto, every nation in Christendom has
supported institutions for teaching the art of war, for
educating expert teachers of the science. But it has
been, until very recently, regarded a duty as well as a
dictate of patriotism, for these normal schools of war
to apply all the military instruction they could impart to
the armies and navies of their own respective countries.
In some cases it has been deemed almost an act of
treason to teach the use of warlike weapons to men who
might turn them against one's own nation. It was a
penal offence, in the early settlement of New England,
to sell fire-arms and ammunition to the Indians. To
teach the Kaffirs, or other barbarous tribes of Africa, the
use of the Minie rifle, would doubtless be regarded as
decidedly unpatriotic by the British Government and
people, even in times of peace. The temptation to sell
such arms at a great profit to the people of foreign
countries has frequently overcome the patriotic scruples
of the manufacturers. Muskets of the Birmingham mark
may be found probably among all the populations of
Christendom, and all the savage tribes of men, who are
likely at any time to become arrayed in battle against
Great Britain. If war were certain to break out between

England and Russia on the first of January next, it is doubtful whether the makers of those celebrated muskets would decline an order for them from the agents of that Power the day before the actual declaration of hostilities, especially if an advance of ten or twenty per cent. were offered on the usual price. When the Oregon controversy between England and the United States was tending to a serious crisis, two enormous Paixhan guns were wrought in England for the American navy. These terrible engines of destruction had such direct reference to the hostile issue of that question, that one was called "The Oregon," the other "The Peace-maker." The latter, however, burst on an amateur trial, and killed on the spot the Secretary of the American Navy and one or two other cabinet ministers. But not the slightest suspicion ever attached to the good faith of the English makers of the great gun. It was believed universally that they did their best to produce an engine of the greatest capacity of destructiveness, in view of the almost moral certainty, that, if ever tested in earnest, it would be first upon the ships of their own nation; that its crater-mouth would pour the first eruption of its iron missiles upon their own countrymen.

But these seeming signs of defective patriotism are charitably ascribed to the law of trade—of demand and supply. Something is pardoned to the spirit and prerogative of commerce, to sell in the dearest and buy in the cheapest market, so long as it is open to all parties.

The manufacturing and material interests of all nations follow this rule. But that governments should get up special international exhibitions of military science, like those of Chobham, Satory, Spandau, and Olmutz, is a novel and anomalous circumstance. It is a curious moral phenomenon, but susceptible, perhaps, of a hopeful interpretation, though involved in a maze of ambiguous meanings. The government of a great nation seems to deem it necessary for its proper defence and security against foreign enemies, to put its army and navy through an extraordinary course of discipline and tactics. Battles "as large as life" are got up day after day, shaking the peaceful country with the unshotted thunder of cannon and the crash of cavalry. But every lesson learned in the art of war is taught with generous courtesy to the generals of those foreign armies which are to be met on the battle-field, should "political events ever make them enemies," to use the language of Napoleon. Nor is the presence of these foreign generals and military professors a mere incident to these occasions. They do not attend them as mere individuals to gratify their personal curiosity. They are regularly delegated by their respective governments to be present, and as well-accredited delegates they are received with the utmost consideration. They are invited to the choicest points of observation, where they can best see the working out of every battle-plan, and the nature and operations of the machinery. They are expected to carry back with them all that can be learned from this normal school of war. All the military advantage which the nation can derive from this exhibition, produced at such cost of money and morals, is shared equally with the countries which are to be its foes, if it ever have any! Here is a novel species of *solidarité*, truly. Here are all the parties that can fight with each other in Christendom, teaching each other gratuitously the art of war! To appreciate the generous eccentricity of this proceeding, it may be helpful to view it side by side with an analogous case. Suppose a dozen gentlemen were for their natural life the sole inhabitants of a distant island in the ocean. Although living by necessity and inclination on good terms generally, they conceive that a case may arise when one must defend himself against the attack of another, or avenge an insult by a duel. They therefore spend a portion of their time in rifle practice and short-sword exercise. Every day they acquire new tact and expertness in the use of these instruments. They seek to make one as keen a marksman or swordsman as the other. But all this dexterity and scientific precision with the rapier and rifle, is to be directed against each other's breasts, in case of any hostile encounter. There are no other persons on the island upon whom they may try their skill. How insane! must be the exclamation of every man of common sense, when called to contemplate such a proceeding as this! But does not this supposed case find a parallel in these

great international exhibitions of the art of war? All
the nations in Europe that can fight with each other,
are here teaching one another the sharp practice of the
sword! This, we say, is a new phase of the military
system of the day. What next? We shall see.

—•—•—

A HAPPY FAMILY.

AMONG the novel sights which throng the streets
of the city of London, for the cheap entertainment of the people, none of them has made a more
pleasant impression on my mind, than a family circle
of different animals and birds, whose deportment is
truly an admirable illustration of the reign of peace.
The proprietor of this novel menagerie calls it, very
appropriately, "The Happy Family." A cage would
be too harsh a name for this place of residence, which
is almost simple enough to be of their own construction.
It is rather a large, square hen-coop, placed on a low
handcart, which the man draws about from one street
to another, and gets a few pennies a day from those
who stop to look at the domestic felicity of his motley
family circle. Perhaps the first thing that strikes the
eye, is a large cat "washing her face," with a dozen
large rats nestling under her like so many kittens, whilst
others are climbing up her back and playing with her

whiskers. In another corner of the room, a dove and hawk are billing and cooing on the head of a dog, which is resting across the neck of a rabbit. The floor is covered with the oddest social circles imaginable. Here weasels and Guinea-pigs, and funny, peeping chickens are putting their noses together caressingly. The slats above are covered with birds whose natural antipathies have been subdued into mutual affection by the law of kindness. For instance, a grave old owl is sitting bolt upright, and meditating in the sun, with a twittering, keen-sighted sparrow perched between his cat ears, and trying to open the eyes of the old sage with its sharp bill. I never pass this establishment without stopping to look at the scene it presents. Its teachings are more eloquent than a hundred lectures on peace and universal brotherhood. I love to see the children stop to look at it; for I know they will carry away a lesson which will do them good; they will think of it on their way to school, and at home too, I hope, when anything crosses their will in the family circle or playground. I could not but wish that this " Happy Family" might be exhibited every morning to all the unhappy human families in the land.

—◦—◦—

JOHN BULL AND OCEAN PENNY POSTAGE.

WE are happy to say, that a new and most interesting agency has been added to our stock of
means for propagating the idea of an Ocean Penny
Postage. An eminent London artist, Henry Anelay,
Esq., to whom we submitted a few lame snatches of the
conception, has presented us an exquisite design, which,
when engraved, must touch the heart of the British public
with lively sympathy for the Ocean Penny Post. We
will merely attempt an outline of the features of this
beautiful thing. John Bull, in the cosiest mood of
grandfatherly benevolence, is represented sitting in an
arm chair, with his squat hat cocked urbanely, and his
yellow-topped boots, looking to the life the image of the
olden time. On one side, a beautiful little fairy of a girl,
with eyes as bright as diamonds, is looking askingly into
his face, while she holds up a letter in one hand, " To
Cousin Jane, in America," and with the other points
toward the American coast, which is dimly seen in the
distance, lined with children black and white, all with
letters in their outstretched hands, and in the act of
hailing an approaching steamer bearing the English flag.
On the other side, a little cherub-headed boy has mounted
the old man's shoulder, and with one of his short, fat

arms about his neck, and the other across his breast, with a letter grasped in his right hand, and with all the cheery faith of a child's heart laughing in his countenance, looks as if he would say, " I shall fetch him now ! " Another lad, of a larger size, in " a shocking bad hat," and trousers which do not reach down to the top of his clumsy shoes by several inches, is standing rather timidly at a bashful distance in front of the chair, holding up a letter in one hand, as if it weighed twenty pounds, and on the open palm of the other a penny, as if it weighed as much.   A little in the background of the group, a sober young chap is seated at a rude bench, trying his first experiment upon the mystery of a letter, and with an expression in his countenance which might be in words, " I'll have a hand in this myself."   The benign old man's face is full of funny suavity, and looks, for all the world, as if the children had really "fetched him."   His hand is plunged promisingly and deeply into his pocket, and his lips are pursed up with that half-ironical, puckering smile of benevolence with which a rich old grandfather gives a penny apiece to half a dozen grandchildren clambering up his knees or tugging at his skirts for a present on a Christmas morning.   At the bottom of the piece these words give language to its significance —" Uncle John ! won't you please send my letter to Cousin Jane, in America, for a penny ? "

In a word, John Bull was never represented to the world in a more agreeable aspect than in this design.

He looks the benign Uncle Toby of the family circle so
to the life, that thousands of children in America, we are
sure, would feel, at the first sight of his face, an inclination to climb up over his big boots into his bosom,
and ask him for a penny. If the children do "fetch
him," so that he shall carry their letters across the ocean
for a penny apiece, his portrait, as sketched in this
picture, will not be too flattering in their estimation,
we trust.

—◦—◦—

THE GROWING IDEA OF A CONGRESS OF NATIONS.

THE present appears to be a very auspicious time
to bring forward the proposition of a Congress
and High Court of Nations. The necessity of an International Tribunal for the legitimate and satisfactory
adjudication of questions of controversy between nations,
is proved by new experience, in the present condition
of Europe. The nations of Europe cannot go to war,
without being foundered, like water-logged ships at sea,
beneath the expenditures which such a war would involve.
Then they all have home difficulties to meet, which must
require all their resources. They are like huge giants,
griped by the cholic, each with his two hands pressed
upon his stomach, to suppress its importunities. They
are not in a condition for fighting, even if they had the

disposition. Now, then, is the time to endeavour to recover the nations of Christendom from the old ruinous system of war, and war establishments in time of peace. We would call upon all the friends of peace and humanity to consider the signs and the facts of the times, to see how the governments of Christendom are in a plastic or reconstructive state. Can we stand by and see them reproduce, and reincorporate in their new policies, the old, barbarous, insane, despotic, and wasteful system of war establishments, which shall go on, as they have done, increasing from year to year, until they reduce the whole of Europe to bankruptcy?

The popular mind, in almost every country, has become alive to the burden of an armed peace system— to its folly and incompatibility with the full development of civil liberty, and with the spirit of the age. What a blessing it would have been to Europe at this juncture, if a Supreme Court of Nations had been erected a year ago, and had been now in session to decide upon the cases of controversy which are threatening to involve half the world in war! We rejoice to see that the proposition of a Congress of Nations is gaining ground in various quarters. One of the most interesting indications of its progress which we have to record, of a late date, may be derived from a speech by Mr. Arnold Ruge, in the German parliament at Frankfort. When the Committee on Foreign Relations presented their report, he moved that the following paragraph be appended thereto:

"That, as an armed peace, by its standing armies, imposes an intolerable burden upon the people of Europe, and endangers civil freedom, we therefore recognize the necessity of calling into existence a Congress of Nations, for the object of effecting a general disarmament of Europe."

In the speech with which he supported this motion he said :

"Peace, universal peace, is commanded by an enlightened humanity, as well as by Christianity. Germany has always been a philosophical nation; and it is but fair that so grand an idea, one so easy to accomplish as this, should be proposed to Europe by Germany. * * The French have ceased to be a conquering people; they will readily join us in forming a Congress of Nations. Fortifications, such as those of Paris, for example, are absurdities, and of no use. In England, too, opinion runs in favour of a Congress of Nations. * * There is no necessity of feeding an army of military idlers and eaters. There is nothing to fear from our neighbouring barbarians, as they are called. You must give up the idea that the French will eat us up, and that the Prussians can eat us up. Soldiers must cease to exist, then shall no more cities be bombarded. These opinions must be kept up and propagated by a Congress of Nations. These opinions will overthrow the military power of Prussia, and if there is to be war, it will be the last, it will be a war against war. * * I vote, therefore, that the nations of Europe disarm at once."

The speaker resumed his seat amidst great applause from a part of the assembly, and from the gallery. We trust that Mr. Ruge will persevere in urging so grand an idea upon the consideration of the German parliament. He has ere this received many letters of congratulation and thanks from various friends of peace in England, which may confirm him in the belief that his views are in harmony with those of thousands on both sides of the Atlantic. He, or any other statesman in Europe, who will take the leadership of this proposition, will find himself supported by a constituency of public sentiment which will surprise the majority of politicians of the present day. Another fact of the times, which is full of promise, is the emancipation of the press on the Continent, and its immediate acessibility to articles on the policy of peace. As an illustration of this, we are grateful to say, that a long article, recently sent from London, developing the proposition of a Congress of Nations, has just been published as a leader in an Italian paper, in Trieste, of a large circulation. Probably six months ago the laws of the country would not have permitted the publication of a paragraph upon the subject, even as a paid advertisement. The same article was also translated into German, and sent for insertion in the *Borsen Halle*, of Hamburgh, and that very important journal gave it a conspicuous place in its columns. Thus the way is open for instituting a simultaneous moral agitation throughout the civilized world in favour of the erection of a well-constructed and permanent High Court of Nations; a proposition which has been discussed by able men in England, France, Germany, and America, for a period of nearly two hundred years. The obstacles which opposed its adoption have been swept away, and its necessity and practicability cannot fail to be recognized by enlightened statesmen of every nation in Europe.

BAGGING WIDOWS' MITES.

THE true-hearted devotion of the poor widow in Scripture, who cast into the treasury her whole substance, made her two-mite gift a richer donation in the SAVIOUR'S eyes than the ostentatious offerings which the rich Pharisees poured in from their stores. There are thousands of poor widows and orphans in this country, who, with hearts full of faith and love, bring their little money-mites to the LORD'S treasury, to contribute to the spread of His gospel of grace and salvation in pagan regions, and in dark places at home. And there is one of the richest governments in the world, that, with a bag under its cloak containing twenty millions of dollars of surplus revenue, and a hooked excise-knife in its right hand, follows these widows and orphans stealthily to the altar of their loving sacrifice, and cuts their mite-offerings in two, dropping the largest halves into its own treasures, to chink feebly between its solid ingots of gold. What a charge! Prove it if you can. We will, by two or three simple facts. A short time ago, a poor missionary among the pagan tribes of Africa, labouring, like his Master, with hardly a place to lay his head, and living on the food of almost savages, sent across the sea a packet of letters directed to different friends in America. It reached New York *viâ* England, charged with five dollars and seventy-five cents postage (£1. 4*s.*) ! Of course, the American Missionary Association, to whose care it was directed, paid this charge, and took it from the office; for they recognized the handwriting of a faithful labourer. But this heavy postage was to be paid out of the little gifts dropped into the treasury of this Christian mission. Here are three items that helped to make up the amount. A poor young woman, in the State of Massachusetts, sent a pair of silver sleeve-buttons, left her by a grandfather, who had worn them sixty years or so. These were the only two mites of the remnant of his fortune, and she thought it would be his wish in heaven that they should go for the gospel to the heathen. The goldsmith valued them at twenty-five cents (1*s.*). The second gift was a dollar from an old man above ninety years of age, in Vermont, who sent it as the last offering he could ever make on earth. Then an afflicted woman in Maine, who had been confined to her couch for years, sent the proceeds of her needlework, at which her lean fingers had plied for twelve months, in the uncertain moments of less acute suffering. And these amounted to three dollars—a gift which it gladdened her heart with gratitude to bestow on the cause she loved. Here, then, there were four dollars and twenty-five cents, contributed in a spirit which the SAVIOUR saw and commended in the widow's donation of two mites. How precious in His sight must have been the thousand thoughts of love and faith associated with these three contributions! The whole sum came almost within a dollar of paying the postage which a government, with a bag of twenty millions of dollars surplus revenue under its cloak, and a hooked excise-knife in its right hand, charged upon the letters of the shoeless missionary of the gospel in Africa to his friends in America! Perhaps some decrepit old woman, with dim eyes and palsied hands, pared and dried apples, or collected mustard-seed enough to make up the full amount demanded at the post office for the little packet he sent across the sea. The American Board for Foreign Missions pay nearly three thousand dollars a year for ocean postage on their correspondence with various missionary stations and persons abroad. Think how many hundreds of little gifts, like those described, are yearly swallowed up by this heavy postal charge on missionary intelligence. Let every one, then, who loves the cause of missions, ask for an Ocean Penny Postage.

—o—o—

THE END OF THAT WAY.

THE most brilliant genius and talents are no protection or safeguard against the fascinating and fettering power of strong drink. In every age, and in every country, learned, eloquent, and high-born men have fallen before this insidious tempter and destroyer of the human race. These high qualities, so much admired and coveted by all classes of the community, do not rescue the victim of this foe, when once entangled in the meshes of its fascination. The height from which the gifted fall, when they sink into the lowest depths of intemperance, measures their misery to the eye of the spectator. We see in their fate the magnitude of the ruin which may be wrought by strong drink. We see how the strongest men are made weak before the intoxicating cup. Before this great enemy of man, as before the king of terrors, the learned and illiterate, the artisan and statesman, the rich and poor, seem to be on an equal footing. There is no safety for either in a moment's dalliance with the tempter. Keep him at a distance. It is dangerous even to "look at the wine when it is red, and when it giveth its colour in the cup." The other day our landlady related to us an incident which illustrates the weakness of men of strong intellects and brilliant talents, when once they have yielded to the seductions of intoxicating drink. This was her simple story:

One day, while at dinner, the servant came running into the room, in breathless haste, saying that there was a poor woman in the yard in a fit. She immediately arose from the table, accompanied by the inmates of her house, in great trepidation and alarm. Immediately before the door a harrowing spectacle of misery met their view. A woman, apparently of middle age, covered with only one thin, tattered, and filthy garment, with all the features of her womanhood distorted with the throes of dissolution, lay gasping with her head against a post. By her side a poor drivelling man stood, swaying to and fro in a blear-eyed stupor, ragged, bloated, and nearly speechless. A little girl, five years of age—a pale thing, without shoes or bonnet, haggard, dirty, and wretched— was kneeling by its mother, with its emaciated, cold arms about her neck, crying bitterly, and begging her to come back to life again. This little girl had been taught to beg by those parents in the first lesson in articulate speech. Oh, it was sad and sickening! The first words she had been taught to frame with her baby-tongue were wicked words of fraud and mendicity. The earliest training of her little hands was to hold them out to those who passed by for pennies. And who was that father who could thus teach these words and arts of deception to his daughter? In what low lane of sin was he born and bred? Had he been taught such lessons in his boyhood? Had he never been inside of a Sunday school? Had he never listened to the voice of religious instruction from the pulpit? Alas! he had filled a pulpit himself, as a preacher, learned and eloquent. He had been a gifted man, of brilliant genius and intellect. That tongue, that now could hardly frame an utterance in its vernacular language, was once fluent in Latin, Greek, and Hebrew. He once stood high as a clergyman of the Established Church of England; and a large congregation, of all ages, had once hung upon those lips, now so chapped, thick, and speechless. That wife, over whom he now bent with his dull, sodden, bloodshot eyes, as she writhed in the last stage of *delirium tremens*, was the daughter of a colonel in the British army, born and bred among all the refinements of cultivated society. The little daughter, sobbing on her bosom, was the child of their hopes, when they spanned with their brilliant iris the first and purest years of their wedded life. Her little feet and hands were now worn to skeleton leanness by her trade of beggary. That voice, which might have been the music of joy in the happiest home, had been trained to win alms by its sweet infantile cadence. While she gnawed the crudest vegetables to appease her hunger, all she gained by begging was swallowed in gin by her wretched parents. And this was their end. The mother died a few minutes after being removed into the hall of the house. The father was removed to the almshouse, where he survived only a few weeks. The little child found home and friends in a charitable institution, where she was cared for with the greatest tenderness. The matron became a mother to her in the sympathies of maternal affection. She wrote to the little orphan's relatives in England, who sent for her to return to them. The day our landlady related this story of her life she left for Philadelphia, to take steamer for Liverpool. The kind matron accom-

panied her as far as Philadelphia, to see her well cared
for on board the ship; and while we write these lines,
the child is on her ocean voyage to the home of her
mother's childhood. What a lesson to the most gifted
intellects is the life of this little one! Who can with
safety "look at the wine when it is red, and when it
giveth its colour in the cup?"

—o—o—

THE SILKEN TIES THAT BIND TWO WILLING NATIONS.

PENDING the discussion of the recent "Oregon
Question," thousands and thousands of good
people, of the two kindred nations, communed together
across the Atlantic, through the medium of "Friendly
International Addresses." One of the most remarkable
of these friendly communications, was the address of
more than sixteen hundred women of Exeter to the
women of Philadelphia and of the United States generally.
This peace-breathing message from the women of Exeter
to their sisters in America, constitutes the most interesting fact and feature of this social movement. It has
been received in the spirit it breathes, and has inspired
a response which will tend to bring over the surges of
human passions the influence of woman, as another
gospel of peace. It was a moment of no ordinary sig-

nificance to the moral world, when the address of the
women of Exeter, with its sixteen hundred signatures,
was exhibited in a public meeting of several hundreds
of their sisters in Philadelphia.

As that album of peace, ten yards in length, was
unrolled from the speaker's desk, until it reached half-
way down the hall, sympathies, that heaven has made
its Æolian harpstrings here on earth, were touched to
the finest issues of their inspiration. A response was
immediately adopted, to use the language of a distinguished lady of that city, "with an earnestness and zeal
which gave evidence that it was a heartfelt utterance;
and its three thousand five hundred and twenty-five signatures, with the one thousand six hundred and twenty-
three from England, encourage the hope that woman is
awakening to her highest duties and holiest hopes;
that she is learning the purifying and blessed influences
she may gain and maintain over the intellect and
affections of the human mind."

The white glove of peace, thus thrown across the
ocean by sixteen hundred Englishwomen, at a time when
strong thoughts were gathering blackness, is now passing
from river to mountain, from valley to valley, and from
prairie to prairie, over the American Union; and woman
is everywhere entering the lists, sexed with all her attributes, for a holy crusade against the fell spirit of war.
All hail to her advent to this field of philanthropy!
Here is a work for the finest qualities of her nature.

Here is a field wherein she may work like an angel, and sing like an angel, " Peace on earth, and good-will to men." Here she may sow the green memorials of her love, and breathe the foliage and taste the fruits of that spirit which, in all the latitudes of humanity and in the cycles of time and eternity, can bring forth naught else than " love, joy, peace, long-suffering, gentleness, goodness, faith, meekness, and temperance." To her who bathed the feet of her LORD with her tears, and wiped them away, as they fell, with the hairs of her head, an everlasting memorial was promised, an affectionate remembrance which should co-exist and co-extend with the gospel of peace. Wherever this gospel has been preached for the last eighteen centuries, this promise has been verified to the mention and remembrance of that act of female sensibility and sympathy and enduring affection. When " the knowledge of GOD shall cover the earth as the waters the sea," and the light of His gospel as the light of the sun, the memorial of that woman's deed will be fulfilled. But there is a similar memorial promised to acts of similar spirit, " done unto the least of these little ones," recognized by a common FATHER as His children, irrespective of clime, colour, or condition. Through these, woman may do all that Mary did unto Him whose feet she washed with her tears.

—o—o—

THE GREAT PEACE CONGRESS AT PARIS.

AND we are now on the retrospective side of this great event. It has gone, with its week of years, into the fixed condition of history. Time's ceaseless shuttle is weaving it further and further into the warp and woof of the past. The future of fifty yesterdays is already between it and us; and the future of fifty to-morrows will, ere long, widen the interval. And were it a childless fact, with no promise of posterity, it might some day die from the memory of the living. But neither principalities nor powers, nor any creature on this earth's face, can separate that fact from its inalienable future, or break the right line of its sequence or continuation. It was an illustrious, but not a meteoric event, first to dazzle, then to darken the vision of those who beheld it. Its light revealed its path of progress, past and future; and not only its path, but its ratio of progression. And it was as clear as the sun, and inevitable as the simplest conviction of sense, that this progression had been, was, and was to be, geometrical, to the full consummation and glory of the idea and condition of peace and brotherhood. There were those present who could tread back that path to the smallest day of small things in the history of this idea—to its little upper room conception in the minds of a few earnest men, who stood up and took twenty years of the world's ridicule or pity for their faith, without blushing or any misgiving whatever. These were not the pioneers of peace, but their first disciples, who took their first lessons from Worcester, Ladd, and others, across the family board, or whilst seated around the parlour fire. They were the second in the order of those who have been permitted to see "a good time coming" from that Pisgah of new revelation, the Mount of Olives. And the idea of universal peace and brotherhood which had arrived at its august inauguration in Paris, as a world's movement, was spread out before them, like a stream widening from the thread-like rill to a mighty river.

How natural and inevitable that they should, at such a moment, revert in their minds to certain progress-points in the cause! How natural it was to look to the first time that the cause was brought down from its little upper-room nursery, and held up, in its ideal state, to a small public meeting! And there was one member of the Congress in Paris, an American delegate, the Rev. Joseph Allen, of Massachusetts, who was present at the first peace meeting ever held on that side of the ocean, or, perhaps, in the world. It was convened on a cold, inclement evening, in the month of November, 1815, in the vestry of a chapel in Boston. There and then a handful discussed the morality of that system of violence which had just reaped its last harvest of human slaughter

on the field of Waterloo. While the entire world was
still rocking, as it were, with the thunder of battle, they
conferred together, with tremulous faith, upon the possibility of banishing war for ever from the earth. That
was a stage in the movement easily to be remembered
at Paris by one who had witnessed it. Then the organization of the first Peace Society in America, or in
England, was another stage of progression, of natural
and pleasant recurrence to the mind. Then the twenty-
five sowing years followed, like a dream of time ; and
at their expiration came the first World's Peace Convention, held in London in 1843, at which there were
present a goodly number of the friends of the cause
from England, the United States, and a few from the
Continent. The idea of permanent and universal peace
seemed to expand into a practicability, and to be animate
with warmer inspiration, as they discussed it in different tongues. At the conclusion of their deliberations,
they ventured to invite the public into the great Exeter
Hall, to hear the new doctrine ; and the people came by
hundreds, and listened to it gladly, and even two or
three members of the British Parliament came in, and
addressed the assembly in favour of the cause. That
was another, an advanced stage of progress. To contrast
it with the little conventicles of the friends of peace, in
the first years of their experience, it seemed a far-reaching
term of a geometrical progression.

Then succeeded five years of educational activities, of

sowing more profusely and broadcast the seed-principles
of human brotherhood among the communities on both
sides of the Atlantic. And another great harvest-day
came. For the first time in the history of the cause,
the friends of peace raised their white banner on the
Continent of Europe, even at a time when the bestial
emblems of antagonist nationalities were floating in
mutual defiance on the breeze. Many true but timid
friends thought it hazardous and unwise to make the
venture in face of such inauspicious aspects. "Wait
until the clouds, that seem reddening with anger, be
overblown; wait until affairs are more settled;" were
the counsels dictated by their solicitude and prudence.
But what if the children of this world should do the
same in their day and generation! What if the hireling
soldiers of brute force should wait for soft skies, and
balmy breezes, and flowery fields, in order to prove their
prowess and courage! No; if "Peace has her victories
no less than War," she has her courage too, as well as
her bloody antagonist—courage to do and endure. And
animated with that courage, the men of peace unfurled
her banner at Brussels, on the 21st of September, 1848.
Then it was that a more novel expedition than Jason's
after the golden fleece was witnessed by the world, as
an *avant-courier* of a new era in the social history of
nations. Never, since "the Spirit of GOD first moved
upon the surface of the waters," did they bear upon
their bosom a more precious enterprise than that of the

steamer "Giraffe," which conveyed across the English
Channel one hundred and fifty missionaries of peace
from Britain to the Congress in Brussels; for the world
would have it that it was a congress, although those who
constituted it tried to call it a convention. And that
Congress was virtually organized in the palace of the
prime minister of Belgium; and men high in office, and
in the estimation of the Belgian Government, took a
leading part in the great demonstration. On one side
of the president sat a member of the British Parliament,
as vice-president for England; on the other, a member
of the French National Assembly, as vice-president for
France. For two days the principles of peace were discussed in a beautiful spirit of fraternal sympathy, and
the decisions of the Congress were clear and unanimous.

And who that was present on this grand occasion
could fail to be impressed with the conviction, that the
cause had advanced by a ratio of geometrical progression
since the convention in 1843? And what wonder that
this and kindred convictions inspired the friends of
peace in England and America with new hopes and
activities! What wonder that it was decided on the
spot, that another Congress should be held the next
year, and at Paris, or some other continental metropolis!
And did not this idea in itself fix a series of geometrical
progression? A Peace Congress every year! Annual
peace-parliaments of the people! Yes; in that idea
there was progress of intense acceleration.

But what was to come in the interval, between the two congresses? Why, twenty years of sowing were to be compressed within the space of six months. Such a movement as the world never saw, to indoctrinate a nation's heart with the principles of peace, was set on foot in England. During that period, more than one hundred and fifty public meetings were held in the kingdom, and more than one thousand petitions were presented to Parliament in favour of arbitration instead of war, signed by two hundred thousand persons. Then, as the consummation of this agitation, came the magnificent and momentous debate on Cobden's motion, at a moment when continental Europe was rocking with revolutionary emotion. And eighty members voted with that premier of common sense for stipulated arbitration; and these represented the largest constituencies in the empire! And there were those who went out with him, who could remember that a proposition, or petition, for establishing permanent and universal peace was received in that house with shouts of laughter. Was there not geometrical progression here?

Well, what next? Why, almost before the issue of Cobden's motion was known throughout England, delegates were being appointed to the great Congress in Paris. And, on the 22nd of August, that august demonstration inaugurated a mighty event in the French metropolis. Two steamers, freighted to the full with the heart and hand of English philanthropy, had conveyed

across the Channel such a host as never before landed
on a foreign shore. Seven hundred strong, they entered
the martial capital of France, to raise aloft, amid its
ensigns of war, the white banner of peace and brotherhood. On their way, they walked over all the rigid
restrictions that hedged about the nation. The custom-
house, octroi, police, and passport, the siege of the city
even suspended their inquisitions, and opened wide their
doors to let the strangers pass. The preventions imposed upon public meetings, upon the press, and the
people, were raised, to let the men of peace speak to
the world from the centre of European civilization. And
when they were ready to speak thus to the people, what
a spectacle they presented! Who that witnessed it will
ever displace it in his memory, to make room for an
event fraught with more varied and novel interest? The
brotherhood of nations was represented on the platform
of the hall. Languages, religions, nationalities, and all
the differences that have separated the great communities
of the earth, were there, harmonizing with the idea of
peace and concord, and that, too, on the presidential
bench. In the centre sat the president of the Congress,
one of the most brilliant orators and poets of France,
and a member of its National Assembly. On his right
was the Abbé Deguerry, *curé de la Madeleine*, a most
eloquent representative of the Catholic church, and on
his left the Protestant pastor, orator, and statesman,
Athanase Cocquerel, representing a union of the two

antagonistic creeds under the banner of brotherhood. Then next on the right sat Richard Cobden, and Charles Hindley on the left, vice-presidents for England. Then the chairs for Belgium and Holland were filled by Visschers and Suringar; and at the extreme right sat M. Carové, for Germany, and on the extreme left, Durkee, a member of the United States Congress, from the distant State of Wisconsin. And for three days that hall resounded with the echoes of eloquence that pleaded, with earnest pathos, dazzling brilliance, and irresistible power, for the perpetual peace and union of the peoples. Heart spoke to heart in the voiceless language of a common sympathy. Great and glowing sentiments of human brotherhood were thus comprehended, with all the fervour of their inspiration, although the words in which they were clothed conveyed no meaning to half the assembly. There was something of a Pentecost in that three days' experience. The French understood the English, and the English the French, although each spoke in his own language. And the crowds of the population that thronged the doors, and the entrances, and the streets leading to the hall, seemed to drink in the spirit of the great occasion, and to be affected with the silent and kindly sympathies which it inspired. Cobden spoke his great words of common sense to the world; and four other members of the British Parliament uttered theirs with force and feeling. Victor Hugo spoke a great word for France, a speech of mighty genius and eloquence;

and four other members of the French National Assembly
followed him, with a power that moved the assembly to
deep emotion.　And all the conclusions were clear,
unequivocal, and strong; and carried with a unanimity
full of enthusiasm.　The cheers, long and loud, that
filled the hall, as the last resolution was adopted, were a
spontaneous expression of gladness, that so many hearts
were susceptible of such a unity of sentiment touching
the brotherhood of nations.

Next came the reception of the foreign delegates to
the Congress by the French Minister of Foreign Affairs,
M. de Tocqueville, when six or seven hundred men
of peace, representing nearly all the communities in
England, and several of other countries, assembled in his
palace, and associated it and his position with the august
demonstration in the Salle St. Cecille.　Then followed
the magnificent celebration of the Peace Congress, instituted by the French government at Versailles and
St. Cloud, an entertainment which had hitherto been
confined to the sovereign guests of France.

Now we would ask every doubting or timid friend of
peace, to look back over the progress of the cause
during the last year, and say if it has not advanced
by a ratio of geometrical progression.　Think of it for
a moment.　The Brussels Congress, the great Arbitration
movement in England, and the noble demonstration in
Paris, all transpired within the space of eleven months !
Contrast the progress of those eleven months with that

of the preceding eleven years, and see if it has not proved that we are reaching onward to the grand consummation of the cause by an intense ratio of geometrical progression !

—o—o—

THE FISHERS OF MEN
AND THE EXPECTATION OF THE WORLD.

FOLLOW me to the shores of the little sea of Galilee. Here the din of battle and clash of arms do not disturb nor redden the placid surface of this sequestered lake. Peaceful are those waters, when the blushing twilight looks down upon them from among the waning stars, or when they slumber in the listless silence of the noontide heat. The stroke of the fisherman's oar, as he trails his net from the cabin-covered beach, or the echo of his voice as he calls to his fellow on the shore, is the only sound that makes the deep silence audible. Can this be the stage, the incipient scene of a momentous revolution? Are any of these poor Galileans, whose only patrimony is their father's nets, to stir the world with deeds and doctrines that shall turn and overturn, until all the kingdoms of the earth shall be consolidated into one grand and everlasting empire? Are these to pluck down kings and thrones, demolish kingdoms and principalities, level altars, depose idols, dethrone gods, break down temples, and raze to the ground every high

place where man has been sacrificed to his fellow?
Are these the men who are to rescue the race from
the tyranny and degradation of their servitude, and rein-
state man in the original dignity of his being and
destiny? Even so! and those two sunburnt peasants
who are letting out their nets from yonder skiff, are to
be the Alexanders and Cæsars in this great conquest
of the world.

Let us contemplate briefly the character and career of
the eldest of these two fishermen. Like his fellows, the
sturdy Galilean knows but little of what has transpired
and is still enacting upon the stormy theatre of the
great world. The rise and fall of kingdoms move him
less than the breath of the autumn gale, which rocks
too roughly his half-anchored skiff. Let Alexander and
Cæsar add another province to their empire at each
wheel of their battalions, the stalwart "son of Jona"
does as much for his ambition at every draught of his
net. What Leander did in the Hellespont, he would do
thrice in the waters of that lake, to carry back a better
filled basket to his cabin on the shore. All that the
unlettered peasant knows of the history of his own
nation, has come to his ears through the vague traditions
of his fathers. He forgets that his country is reduced
to a Roman province, except when some odious publican
reminds him that " Cæsar Augustus has decreed that all
the world shall be taxed." True, he has often heard
snatches of his country's history read by some itinerant

scribe; how his ancestors served and sojourned in Egypt, and how they returned to the land where their dispirited descendants are now almost strangers. He has heard of David and Solomon, and all the illustrious kings of Israel and Judah, that made the nations tremble with their prowess. He has heard that long and bitter story told of the Babylonish captivity; of the destruction of Jerusalem, the desolation of Mount Zion, the return from Chaldea, and most of the subsequent trials and tribulations which have reduced the Jews to their present oppressed and degraded state. Like every other peasant in Israel, he could recite the promises and predictions of the prophets concerning the advent of the MESSIAH who is to reign upon the throne of David with a majesty that shall overawe the world.

Every variety of metaphor has been employed to describe the glory, extent, and duration of this kingdom. While the captive Israelites were wandering through the land of their exile; while, at the remembrance of their demolished Temple, their harps fell from their hands, and their tears mingled with the cold streams of Babylon, some grey-headed pilgrim-prophet of GOD would take up a song of Zion, and while his tremulous voice lingered upon its melting strains, he would sing the glories of that future kingdom, until every captive's heart beat again with joyful expectation.

And the long expected day drew near. They had borne the yoke of almost every surrounding nation; they

H

had been stripped, and peeled, and mocked, and ridiculed by the Gentiles. For five hundred years they had been spoiled and wasted by the Persians, Macedonians, Syrians, Egyptians, Arabians, Parthians, and Romans. The pagans of every region had hated them for their religion; and they had suffered every species of persecution in adhering to the institutions which GOD had given them. No people on earth had ever given such proofs of fidelity to their religion and laws. All the efforts of Antiochus and Ptolemy to impose upon them idolatry were in vain. These Egyptian and Syrian monarchs had let loose upon them their pagan minions, and offered no alternative between idol worship and utter extermination. Their sacred books were burnt, and their ordinances abolished. The Syrian soldiers, like the military missionaries of Louis XIV, had entered every dwelling in Judea, and presented on the point of the sword paganism or death. Children of widowed mothers, who had scarcely received the ordinance of consecration to GOD, had been carried through the streets of Jerusalem suspended by the neck upon poles, and then dashed over the highest ramparts of the city upon the rocks below. Armies had encamped round about Jerusalem; and all the slave-dealers of the east had followed in their train, to buy, at a preconcerted price, all that the extirpating sword should spare of that hated race. Still, with strong, undaunted hearts, they sent up the morning and evening sacrifice from the caves of the mountains, and from their hiding-places in the forest and desert. Thousands raised their expiring eyes toward Jerusalem, and breathed forth their last prayer towards its beloved, though profaned Temple, even while transfixed by the spears of the relentless pagans. Even their bloodthirsty enemies tired in this futile war against their religion, and were confounded at the impregnable endurance of the human soul. Monarchs that had subjugated and divided the world could not separate this handful of Israelites from the institutions of their fathers. They clung to them with increasing tenacity among the tortures of a pagan inquisition. While resisting unto blood for their holy religion, no crisis could induce them to violate a single ordinance of Moses; and the soldiers of Antiochus, Ptolemy, and Pompey butchered them by thousands on the sabbath, because they would not lift their hands in their own defence on that hallowed day.

But the time drew near when the promises and predictions of their final deliverance were to be realized. This glorious hope braced up their hearts against the fierce current of adversities that was overwhelming them. They were soon to have their turn in the great world, and lead captivity captive. They had seen what Nebuchadnezzar and Cæsar had done to the earth: they had been hewers of wood and drawers of water to these gigantic conquerors. But now the day was close at hand when their long expected SHILOH was to sit upon the throne of Solomon, and wield a sceptre that should be recognized and obeyed by nations that should outlive

Chaldea, Persia, Macedon, and Rome. His kingdom
was to be an everlasting empire, reaching "to the
uttermost corners of the earth," and the remotest islands
of the sea. Kingdoms whose Egyptian yoke they had
borne for ages, were to be their willing tributaries. All
the great and petty sovereigns of the world were to
receive their religion and laws at Jerusalem, and become
nursing fathers and mothers, waiting men and maidens
to the institutions of Moses. Under this mighty sceptre,
no Persian, Grecian, Syrian, or Roman chief should lift
a hostile spear, or set a profaning foot upon their holy
mountain. This vast theocratic dynasty was not only to
enforce a universal equity, but righteousness and peace
throughout the world. The puny rage of the heathen
was to be softened down to meek submission before the
august majesty and irresistible power of this great
empire, which should fill the whole earth. The GOD of
Israel was to be known and worshipped in every corner
of the world, and His worshippers defended in their
exercises of devotion by a civil power that should
overawe the blind fury of idolatry.

And what other kingdom than one stronger than the
Roman empire could realize to themselves the religious
privileges which were promised them at the advent of
the MESSIAH? While, sixty years before the birth
of CHRIST, the soldiers of Pompey were butchering
the unresisting Jews by thousands in their Temple on the
sabbath, what other than such a kingdom could those

priests have expected, when, with untrembling hands and voice, they stood by the altar, and offered incense to their fathers' GOD, amid the smoking blood of their brethren, wives, and children, who were massacred at their sides? What lacked they at that hour, but a kingdom that should wrest from the raging heathen the sword of persecution, and let the pagan world know, by awful demonstration, that there was still a GOD and KING in Israel? Was their devotion defective and formal in that dreadful scene?—were they worshipping graven images there? No! The history of religion—even the strong tenacity of Egyptian superstition—does not furnish a parallel to the fidelity of these Jews to the institutions which they had been commanded to observe. Was not the religion of Moses to be the religion of their MESSIAH? Were the statutes, precepts, and ordinances of GOD to be commuted or rendered obsolete under this great LAWGIVER and PRINCE, who was to establish all things? Were the laws of Mount Sinai to be abrogated, and replaced by a moral code more genial to the pagan world and human heart? Were their venerable and hallowed institutions to give place to forms of worship less imposing and impressive, or less obnoxious to the taste of the Gentiles? If not, how then was the worship of the only true GOD, the GOD of Israel, to be propagated through the world, without the co-operation of a temporal power that should protect His worshippers? Without the intervention of such a government, how was their divine religion to prevail at Rome, Athens, Alexandria, and the remote cities of Asia, when even in the acropolis of Jerusalem, in the very Mount Sion of GOD, the name of JEHOVAH was interdicted by the sword? For ages they had been wading along in civil impotence through seas of bitter persecution, merely because they clung with unshaken fidelity to a religion which the world hated, and was determined to destroy. How then could they hope that this religion, from its own innate and essential excellence and power, would prevail at the courts of heathen emperors and sovereigns, when they could hardly find a recess deep and dark enough in the deserts of Judea, to observe its simplest ordinances unmolested? They had no such hope — such an expectation seemed absolutely precluded. Taking the political, religious, and intellectual character of the world into consideration, not even the aged Simeon himself, who was waiting for the consolation of Israel, when the child JESUS was brought into the Temple, could have thought the infant he held in his arms could be the glory of His people Israel, or a light to lighten the Gentiles, without being, at the same time, a great temporal prince, as well as a divine SAVIOUR.

Not only were their own sacred writings full of the predictions of such a kingdom, but Persia, Greece, and Rome were filled with sibylline prophecies of an event which coincided with the impression of the Jews. It would compass no part of our design to inquire or

ascertain how these mysterious intimations of an occurrence predicted by the prophets of Israel crept into the
leaves of the Cumean sibyls. Whether the shadow of
the coming event cast its luminous penumbra over the
night-bound regions of paganism, or whether it was
the purpose of Divine Providence, that the vaticinations
of these female Baalims should predispose the world for
a new era, is a question which we have no need nor
motive to discuss. This much was true: the world was
expecting a new epoch. From the Euphrates to the
Tiber this impression was prevalent and deep; and, with
but a slight variation, it coincided with the impression of
the Jews. Everywhere, He who was to come was to be
the greatest of earthly monarchs, the greatest of earthly
lawgivers and counsellors, the PRINCE of Peace, Righteousness, and Equity. These were the attributes which,
the world conceded, were to characterize Him and His
kingdom. Nations varied somewhat with regard to the
place which should give Him birth; and so did the Jews.
When Rome was in the height of her glory, it was an
opinion cherished in the very court of the Cæsars, that
this exalted personage was to ascend to the throne of
that empire. They had raised Cæsar Augustus to the
rank and dignity of a demi-god, and erected temples to
his honour all over their domains; but they ascribed far
higher divinity to their pagan Messiah. Julius Marathus,
speaking of his advent, says: "*Regem populo Romano
Naturam parturire;*" or that Nature, or their deity, was

about to bring forth a king to the Roman people ; thus distinguishing his birth by a supernatural divinity from any prince that had as yet wielded the Roman sceptre. When the long, wasting wars, which preceded the accession of Cæsar Augustus to the throne, had ceased, he found the garden of Europe reduced almost to a wilderness. The bloody factions of rival aspirants to a crown had trodden out the honest occupation of agriculture; for the wanton rapine of civil war had driven the husbandman from his field.

Among other expedients to reclaim the country from this artificial sterility, Virgil was induced to lend the aid of his life-inspiring genius. His inimitable Pastorals surpassed their anticipated effect. *Recubans sub tegmine fagi*, his oaten reed summoned spell-bound thousands to the fertile fields of Italy ; and all her vine-clad hills, her rich valleys, her mountains and forests were filled with the joyful echoes of labour, which the poet set to the music of his verse. One of these Pastorals appears to be a poetic version of one of the prophecies of the Cumean sibyl. His very first line indicates his sense of the dignity of the subject, which he thus reverently introduces:

> " Sicelides Musæ, paulo majora canamus :
> Jam redit et Virgo, redeunt Saturnia regna;
> Ultima Cumæi venit jam carminis ætas.
> Magnus ab integro sæclorum nascitur ordo,
> Jam nova progenies cœlo demititur alto.
> Tu modo nascenti puero, quo ferrea primum
> Desinet, ac toto surget gens aurea mundo,
> Casta, fave, Lucina."—*Buc.*, Ecl. iv.

Without submitting these and subsequent lines to the loose fidelity of a metrical version, they may be rendered literally thus:

> "Ye Sicilian muses, some greater themes let us sing:
> Now the Virgin (Astræa) and Saturn's reign return;
> Now comes the last age of the Cumean verse.
> Anew the great order of the ages is born;
> Now a new progeny is sent down from high heaven.
> Thou chaste Lucina, befriend the infant boy
> By whom first the iron age shall end
> And one of gold to the whole world arise."

He next proceeds to describe the character of this new reign, which, be it remembered, he was presenting in a species of contrast with the golden reign of Augustus, in whose dazzling court this poetical prediction was read and sung. In this description, some of his very words seem borrowed from the inspired delineations of the MESSIAH's kingdom.

"Te duce," says he, "every remaining vestige of our guilt, being washed away, shall for ever release the earth from fear. He shall partake of the life of the gods; he shall see heroes mingling with the gods, and he himself be seen of them; and rule the tranquillized world with his father's virtues. And the earth, thou illustrious child, shall without culture yield thee creeping ivy with the lady's glove, the colocasia with the blushing acanthus. The goats of themselves shall homeward bear their milk-distended udders; nor shall the flocks fear the great lions more. The very cradle shall put forth sweet-breathing flowers. The serpent shall die; and the deceitful poisonous plant shall die. The Assyrian spikenard shall grow in every soil. All lands shall bear all things. The ground shall not be worried by the harrow, nor the vineyard by the pruning-hook. The sturdy ploughman shall release his bullocks from the yoke. Nor shall the wool longer learn to counterfeit various colours; but the ram himself shall in the meadows tinge his fleece, now with sweet blushing purple, and now with saffron dye. Scarlet shall clothe spontaneous the lambs. Haste, ye ages so blessed! Bright offspring of the gods, illustrious progeny of Jove, take possession of these signal honours, for the time is close at hand! Behold the round world, the earth, the expanse of ocean, and the high heavens above, are beckoning to thee. See all rejoicing in the coming age! O that my last stage of life may continue so long, and so much breath remain as shall suffice to sing thy deeds!"

Such was the poetical version which Virgil gave of the prophecy of the Cumean sibyl with respect to the new era, which was to be introduced by one who was to come. In other parts of the world the same idea prevailed with but a slight modification.

Suetonius, in speaking of that period, affirms, that there was an ancient opinion generally and steadfastly entertained throughout the East, "that fate had decreed that about that time, there should arise out of Judea those who should attain to the empire of the world." And those oriental magi who first descried the star of Bethlehem, had probably been watching for that celestial signal for years. And when, after their long pilgrimage to Judea, they bowed in adoration to the infant king of the Jews, they recognized and worshipped in Him the future monarch of the earth; for they would not have gone a mile to see the heir apparent to the throne of such a little desolate territory as Judea.

Whether the migratory Jews, who were dispersed in

every city and nation, had any influence in producing this general presentiment, is a question irrelevant to the point under consideration. This much was true. The world was waiting for such an event, in a remarkable attitude. The doors of the temple of Janus at Rome swung back upon their rusty hinges, and war rested pensive and wearied upon its inverted spear. The Roman soldier unbuckled his hacked helmet and shield, and poised the spade and the mattock. At the tail of the plough, he marched to the matin tune of the lark through fields which, all stained with human blood, hid their blushing face beneath a thicket of weeds.

The fierce, indomitable Parthians sent back the captured eagles of Rome, and ceased to taunt the generals of Augustus with the fate of Crassus and Anthony. The Syrian and Egyptian met no longer in angry parlance upon the plains of Philistia. The clash of arms died away upon the banks of the Tagus, the Seine, the Rhine, and the Danube. The Briton, the Gaul, and the Goth carried back each his war-club from the field, and hung up his quiver again in his cabin. The Northman left the track of the Roman, and followed that of the white bear over his own sunless mountains of snow. The wild Scythian resumed the shepherd's crook, and drove his flocks over the unfenced pastures of the East. A supernatural calm came over the boisterous surges of the world, and all was still.

It was still in Judea ; still upon the little sea of

Galilee, when Peter and Andrew pushed out from the shore on that quiet morning. If the two unlettered peasants were ignorant of the signs of the times, they were not ignorant of the general expectation of Israel; and each felt a personal interest in their nation's hope. While silently gathering in their scanty draught of fish, perhaps they were, at that moment, revolving in their minds, in what way the reign of the promised MESSIAH would affect their interest and occupation. The youngest, perhaps, was dwelling upon the vision of a larger cabin in the hill country of Judea, surrounded by his own vines and fig-trees; or even of a richer dwelling on the fertile plains of the Jordan. His brother Simon, less inclined to the peaceful monotony of rural life, might have been wondering if he should not be promoted to some civil or military station under this illustrious reign, that he might bring into play the natural energy of his character, and do the state some service in the great expansion of the Jewish empire.

They were diverting the sense of their toil with thoughts like these, when the sound of a footstep on the beach fell upon their ears. They started upon their feet to see a stranger walking alone upon that lonely shore. The stranger came alone; he wore no badge of Roman nobility; he held no commission from Cæsar Augustus. He had no air of human authority in his carriage or countenance. He had no credentials from Herod or the high-priest; no outward pretension to rank. His hands bore the impress of the axe and the adze; for he had been a faithful apprentice to a carpenter, and had built many a cottage in his native village. No overawing majesty of bearing declared the prince; no expression of royal dignity shone in his eye or sat on his lip. No rigid austerity nor tone of command took away the silvery sweetness of his voice, when, abreast of their skiff, he paused and uttered that simple sentence: "Follow me, and I will make you fishers of men. And they left all, and followed him."

THE ANARCHY OF GOVERNMENTS.

WHAT are the aim and upshot of the measures proposed by the friends of peace? What do they expect to accomplish by arbitration treaties, or by an annual Peace Congress at Paris, Brussels, or Frankfort? Would they break down all the defences of law and order, and give anarchy a *carte blanche* to riot, to the full of its frenzy, upon the ruins of society? To these questions, which embody the current charges of fanaticism and other hallucinations, we would reply, that the friends of peace claim to be "the friends of order" in a more honest and extensive sense than is usually adopted by those who are so fond of arrogating to themselves this title. What is the aim of their operations ? It is to cut the sinews of anarchy, by reducing governments themselves to law and order in their intercourse with each other; to constrain parliaments and national legislatures to do homage to the principles of justice and equity, for which they exact unswerving loyalty from their own subjects or citizens. The recent events which have filled continental Europe with emotion, solicitude, and alarm, have been collisions of the peoples with their governments — the uprising of great communities against the authorities and institutions under which they had lived, in some cases, for centuries. The great capitals of the Continent have been the theatres of violence and bloodshed. During the darkness of a single night, their streets have been walled through and through with barricades, bristling with weapons of murderous warfare, wielded with fatal dexterity by the very scavengers and chimney-sweeps of their respective populations. But who taught these masses of the populace to construct barricades in the darkest hours of the night with such military skill ? Who taught them the terrible tactics of a bloody revolution—the science of attack, defence, fortification, and all the mysteries of martial movements ? Who taught these men of the spade, pickaxe, and shovel; and these men of the needle, spindle, and easel; of the hod, hedgebill, and hammer— who taught these to point cannon, spring mines, and beat back long-trained regiments of the line with their own weapons ? Whence have these men in blouses, smock-frocks, and fustian jackets, all this dangerous teaching? Did they derive it from their various occupations? Did the pickaxe, spade, trowel, spindle, or any other honest implements suggest such lessons as these, whilst employed in honest labour? No, never! It is true — and shame to the civilization of the age that it is true — this military education of the masses is the only gratuitous education which the governments of the civilized world guarantee to the populations committed to their care. It is the inevitable and universal education of the war system in time of peace. The barricades of 1848 were only the seeds of the barracks of the standing army, suddenly developed into the full ear of crime by the passions of an inflamed populace. They were nearly all erected in walled cities, whose bastions and armaments were a standing lesson of military science to the masses which they were to defend or overawe.

But the use and tactics of brute force are the slightest lesson which the governments of the civilized world are gratuitously teaching their subjects through the war system. There is still a lesson of deeper demoralization, of deadlier peril to the internal peace and order of nations, which results from this system, and that is, the lesson in the spirit of violence which a government gives to its subjects, when it kindles the desolating flames of war to settle any question of disputed right, honour, or interest.

What crime has assumed more turpitude and peril

in the eyes of those who call themselves "the friends
of order," than that which has been perpetrated by
individuals and communities, who, to use a term which
is thought to describe the act, have "taken the law into
their own hands ?" In every civilized country, the man
who takes even a well-defined law of the land into his
own hands, or makes himself its judge, and pronounces
and executes its legitimate penalty upon an individual
who has wronged him, violates the first principles of
justice and order, which can never permit personal
passions or interests to influence either judge, jury, or
witness. But if there be one act which, more than
another, is regarded as high treason to order, it is that
act by which a mob or a populace attempt to extemporize and execute, in the same moment, the law of their
own ignited passions by sheer brute force; or, in other
words, to establish right by might. And it is these
fearful violations of order which have filled continental
Europe with consternation and dismay during the past
few years. But have not the populations guilty of this
crime derived no precedents for their madness and folly
from the practice of their own governments ? When a
nation or its government "cries havoc, and lets slip the
dogs of war," does it not "take the law into its own
hand" with a vengeance ? Nay, more, does it not
extemporize and execute simultaneously the law of un-
leased passions, of sheer brute force, with all the madness and unsparing cruelty of a mob ? There is often,

in the practice of war something more inhuman and unjust than is found in acts of popular violence.

The maddened masses, in the climax of their fury, generally retain some sense of distinction between the different orders of wrong or grievance against which they fancy they are contending. In the most lawless countries, a mob seldom burns a man's house for debt, or hangs him on the first tree to settle a question of disputed territory, or even to avenge an aggravated insult. But all distinctions in crime are swallowed up in the bloody judgment of war. For war never inflicts anything short of capital punishment for any crime, however low in the scale of guilt. According to the morality of its inhuman system, a government may carry fire and sword through a neighbouring country, either to collect a national debt, avenge a national insult, or establish the right to a disputed territory. It may deal out as much desolation and ruin for the possession of an oaken bucket as for that of an empire.

How, then, can governments expect an unbroken reign of order at home, when they themselves are living in a state of international anarchy? How can they expect undisturbed peace and quietness within their own borders, whilst they are sedulously teaching their subjects, not only the use and tactics of brute force, but the worst spirit of violence, through the medium of a war system, which is almost enough to "make a wise man mad," by the oppressive taxes which it imposes upon the

I

industrial populations which are compelled to bear the brunt of the burden?

The Utopias of the friends of peace have this extent, no more—to bind our governments themselves to keep the peace; to induce them, in their mutual dealings, to set an example of good behaviour to their own subjects. A treaty of international arbitration is only one of the bonds which we would ask governments to give, in the face of the civilized world, that they will not hereafter break the peace, by taking the law into their own hands, after the spirit and fashion of mobs; that they will not, by resorting to war, kindle a huge and fiery rebellion against the first principles of order, justice, and humanity; that they will not set these terrible examples of violence to their own subjects, thus planting a volcano of passions in the bosom of every nation, ready to burst forth and upturn the foundations of its society, at the slightest popular emotion. This is the prime object of the Peace Congresses which we propose to hold from year to year. To reduce governments to law and order; to recover them from their present state of international anarchy, will be the prime object of all the Peace Parliaments of the people, which we hope to see assembled annually in Europe, until the bloody arbitrament of war shall be recorded among the *effête* barbarisms of a pagan age.

—◦—◦—

THE GUIDE LIGHT OF THE GOSPEL.

AS, in the structure and productive capacity of our globe, and the constitution of man, there was a consentaneous provision for the continued propagation and sustenance of the human family; so all the revelations of nature and of the Bible have been, are, and will be made for man in a progressive state. This state is the inevitable condition of his being; and everything in heaven above or on the earth beneath, designed to facilitate his destiny, was created in as much conformity to this state of progression as the eye to the light and the light to the eye. The gospel not only recognizes this progressive tendency of the human mind, but, above all the revelations made to man, its principles were adapted to promote and perpetuate it to the end of time. It contains lessons of wisdom for the first man, in the very infancy of thought; and for the last man on earth, in all the immense capacity to advance, to improve, to accelerate the moral progress of intellectual beings. It is the text-book of GOD given to humanity, with precepts apportioned to every age, to every condition, to every grade of human advancement. It had a lesson reduced to the comprehension of the unweaned intellect of Adam, embodying an element of improve-

ment and progress; it had another, in the geometrical
series, for Noah, and Abraham, and Moses, and David,
and Daniel. And for the first-born, for " the least in
the kingdom of heaven," for the lowliest peasant that
listened to the teachings of the SON OF GOD, or was
commissioned to carry them to the end of the world, it
had another lesson, embodying the aggregate wisdom of
all the lessons taught or learned in the previous annals
of mankind, superadded to that which, in the language of
our SAVIOUR, made the least in His kingdom of grace
greater than Solomon or Daniel. The era of the gospel
constituted an era in the history of mankind—a point in
its steady progression, where its subsequent advancement
was to be accelerated by the intense ratio of geometrical
gradation. Absorbing all the indistinct and glimmering
rays of previous revelation, it arose in the murky firmament of the moral world, a sun which has never set—
never will set—never reach its meridian ; but which has
shone on brighter and brighter, from the hour that its
morning beams radiated from the lowly birth-place of
its eternal Author to this favoured day of its diffusive
light. If, then, by constitutional necessity, the human
mind has ever been and ever must be in a state of
progression; and if the genius of the gospel not only
conforms, but most intensely conduces to that state ;
how, then, can any one walking by its light, living by its
precepts, and breathing its spirit, stand in the same
footprints that he occupied last year? But, above all,

how can he stand in the same position with regard to any moral question, as that taken by remote predecessors of a former age? With the increasing light of GOD'S Word shining around his path of duty, must he go back into the starlight of the past, for precedents or traditionary customs to direct his course and enlighten his convictions? When called to act in view of a new condition of society and of new duties resulting therefrom, may he not lay his hand upon the gospel, and say, "A greater than Solomon, or Daniel, or Luther, or Melancthon, or Edwards, is here?" In declining to make their example the rule of his conduct, with regard to moral questions growing out of a new state of things, does he impeach their wisdom and piety? Certainly not, any more than we question the learning and indefatigable industry of Hipparchus, Ptolemy, and Tycho Brahe, when we even sweep away the basis of their theories.

—◦—◦—

WAR'S RELIGION.

WE care not, says this war spirit in effect, how many bibles and missionaries you send abroad in the world. Go; preach your law of love among all the dark habitations of cruelty. Tame down the darkened heart of the savage, till he turn his cheek to the smiter, and the fire of revenge go out in his eye.

Let the fierce cannibals of the Pacific islands inhale the
spirit and precepts of your MASTER, till all their ferocious
impulses are softened down to the kindliest sympathies
of humanity. Set up the standard of the cross on the
banks of every river, on the top of every mountain,
"From Greenland's icy mountains to India's coral
strand." Let the whole heathen world imbibe its
peace-breathing doctrines, till they shall dethrone their
idols, and raze their bloody altars to the ground.
Oppose the whole power of the Christian religion
against the long array of their traditionary customs.
Let the light of the gospel travel as fast and as far as
the light of the sun, and moral darkness, degradation,
and all the night-shades that have gathered for ages
in the firmament of humanity, melt away before its
meliorating beams. Let its conquests embrace all the
passions, and co-extend with the limits of human nature.
Let everything bow to its genial sway; let it uproot
every vice, extirpate every passion, except the war spirit.
Between that and the gospel spirit let there be an
amiable, eternal union. Wedded beneath the sombre
shadows of barbarism, let not modern Christianity seek
to weaken the bonds of their wedlock. In imitation of
pagan usage, war must have a religion. It has had one
in all ages. It is not at all particular about the divinity
or humanity of that religion, if it but inspire the warrior
with a recklessness of human life, and add vivacity to
his ferocious courage. The stone and wooden gods

which the pagans of the old world carried into their battles served them well enough. They fought as bravely as Christians under their patronage, and achieved victories which have hardly been equalled since the Christian era. We never expect to get up better fighting than that which came off at the Pass of Thermopylæ, at Platea, and Marathon. If idolatry were not behind the age, we should desire no better religion for our modern wars than Alexander's; and we doubt not that his was as serviceable in the day of battle as Bonaparte's, or the Duke of Marlborough's, or that which Cortes bore on his sword's point over the walls of Mexico. To come to the point, then: here is a country adjoining ours; it is a goodly territory, and we want it; and we will have it, right or wrong. We will fight for it and wrench it by force from its rightful owners. We expect, in the course of the war, to kill fifty thousand men, sack and burn fifty towns and villages, sink as many ships, destroy one hundred millions of the enemy's property, and get the territory besides.

Now, we doubt not that we could do all this without the patronage of any religion, or even if every soldier in our army were an atheist and denied the immortality of the soul. Or, if necessary to invest the business with some religious colouring, we might import from the catacombs of Egypt a deified lizard, or other reptile, that once ranked high among the Egyptian deities, especially among their battle-gods. Or we might inscribe on our banners the semblance of Jeroboam's calf, and hack in pieces a column of the enemy, or burn a town, or sink a ship, as easily as if marching under the standard of Constantine. Nor would it matter with him who fell, whether the bayonet that split his heart open, or the heel that trod his bloody corpse into the ground belonged to a pagan or Christian. But war, having patronized every species of idolatry and every form of religion from the earliest periods of wooden gods and deified snakes, extends its iron hand fondlingly to the meek-eyed genius of Christianity, wooes her approving smile, and invites her to ride into the rifts of battle upon the cannon's breech; to clamber over breastworks of the dead and dying into murky, sulphur-dripping chasms blown into the walls of a beleaguered city; to dabble in pools of hot human blood with her angel feet, which would have been "beautiful on the mountains," if shod with the preparation of the gospel of peace, instead of iron; to smear her white robe in the red rivulets hissing from quivering heaps of the slain; to alternate with the obstreperous rattle of bass and kettle-drums in a song of Zion, and sing *Te Deum* over the smoking ruins of a city, in horrid concert with the shrieks of widows and orphans and the groans of fathers, brothers, and sons biting the dust in mortal agony; to kneel upon some demolished bastion, slippery with human gore, and with the infernal incense of gunpowder, offer up thanksgiving to the GOD of battles, that, among the trophies of His grace and the triumphs of religion, are numbered a dozen ragged pieces of silk, inwrought with lions, eagles, unicorns, and the like, a thousand muskets still in murdering order, and great cast-iron cannon in fragments or entire, and squadrons of dead horses, and a thousand human bodies—burnt, blackened, mangled bodies—that, an hour before, had immortal souls in them, and hearts capable of an immensity of love, hope, and joy.

To such an *auto-da-fe* war would politely invite the Christian religion: not that she must dwell continually in camps, or confine her presence and inspiration to the field of carnage. O no! while the great war spirit is reposing among its trophies, she may go on the commission she received eighteen centuries ago, and carry the gospel of the meek, loving, forgiving JESUS to the dark corners of the world, to most unilluminated pagans who never witnessed its transforming influence upon a Christian nation.

—o—o—

THE HUSBANDRY OF THE PLOUGH AND THE SWORD.

ENGLAND is the admiration of the world for the high perfection to which it has carried the science of agriculture. To the American traveller, England seems a prize garden, tilled to show the whole world what beauty and wealth labour may produce from a given area

of the earth's surface. Every one of its fields, in seed
time or harvest, looks within its green hedges, like a
framed picture, upon which scores of human hands have
wrought with artistic skill, from the earliest song of the
lark to the last ray of the setting sun.   All its green
and graceful trees, whether grouped in groves or forests,
or ranged like veteran life-guards around a hundred
parks; wherever they stand, whether in the farmer's
hedge, or in the choicest preserve of royalty, they are
all the nurslings or monuments of labour.

All through the year, even in the middle of winter,
labour is abroad with its plough, spade, hedgebill, or
shears, fertilising, beautifying, cutting, or trimming. Go
where you may, you will see the fields, hedges, gardens,
parks, and lawns of England teeming with men, women,
and children toiling to make their country a living
picture of wealth and beauty. And what do they receive
for making it such a picture? What is the sum total
paid for all the toil and skill which make England the
wonder of the world for the productions of its soil and
the rich finish of its landscapes? Why, it is said that
there are seven hundred thousand labourers employed
to do all this work, and that their weekly wages average
ten shillings per head.   Then all the agricultural labour
bestowed upon England, to make it what it was at the
last harvest, cost £18,200,000 a year. Now, then, let
all who looked with delight upon the country in the time
of the golden corn remember; let every one of those

seven hundred thousand labourers, and all the farmers
who paid them, remember, that England this very year
appropriated £18,500,000 to mere husbandry of war—
for mere preparations for blasting, consuming, impover-
ishing war! that she paid more for training men and
instruments to reap down human beings on the battle-
field, than it would cost to till just such another England
to all the perfection of agriculture which their country
could show during the last twelve months! English
farmers! is not this a startling thought for you? Think
of it when you plough, and sow, and reap, and on the
way to market! Think that your country pays more
for hired men to kill their brethren of another country,
than you pay for growing corn and producing food for
ten millions of human beings.

—◦—◦—

TEACHING THE YOUNG IDEA HOW
TO SHOOT.

THE ten years that immediately succeeded the
Declaration of Peace, in 1815, constituted the age
of military bands and bards in the United States—
the great reign of cockades and epaulettes, when those
who had been peaceful citizens during the war became
valorous soldiers, and charged the air with long undu-
lating rows of bayonets, and scorched the trees, and

clouds, and themselves with the villainous saltpetre.
It was the great era of train-band chivalry, when every
able-bodied man was summoned to the parade, to charge
his gun with powder, and himself with rum; when
corporals and other distinguished men did doughty deeds
on the village green, and captured hearts at the head of
sections; when the whole village assembled with beating
hearts, and mothers, with infants in their arms, stood
sweltering in the sun, to see "the trainers;" when the
rustic swain, who had well-nigh lost his suit in his
Sunday clothes, became irresistible in his fair one's eyes,
when he donned the uniform of a train-band Mars.
There is no period of equal duration in our history,
when so many influences co-operated to make the war
spirit the mania of the people. It put old age, manhood,
and infancy under martial law. It turned the nursery
into a little military camp, where the associations, impressions, and objects of war were the first impressed
upon the infant mind. When the little thing nestled
within its bulrush ark, and strained its eyes to see what
kind of a world it was born into, to look for some object
to love, its mother satisfied its yearning instincts with
miniature instruments of war. Its constant companions
were soldiers equipped in pastry; and squadrons of
fierce-looking troopers in sugar guarded its cradle. As
soon as the boy had donned the garments which were
to distinguish his sex, his father celebrated that public
distinction by presenting him a wooden sword, with

several inches of the point painted red, to suggest its bloody design.

At this point of his military education, he was plied with a set of influences which have ceased to exist. In every neighbourhood there were always several Revolutionary soldiers, whose hearts burned within them while recounting from house to house the thrilling reminiscences of that long struggle. And the little fellow stared with ecstasy at those strange stories. Holding on to grandpa's knee, he looked up into his face with startling interest, while the garrulous old man was recounting to a contemporary the dreadful "Fatigue of Burgoyne." How it fired his young heart to see the old man turn the right wing of the British army with his crutch, while the other limping veteran took them in flank with his staff, and routed them horse and foot over a single mug of hard cider! He now begins to have a presentiment that he is to be a man. In his illicit explorations about the kitchen, parlour, and garret, he has discovered his father's gun, his cartridge-box, the red-tipped plume, and particoloured coat. From that moment he looks with sovereign contempt upon his tin and pewter dragoons. He will be pacified with no compromise with his mother or sisters; he spurns with indignation all allusions to the shortness of his legs; he will not be bought off with any promise of larger troopers in wax or wood; he insists upon being led to the parade to see "the trainers." His father acquiesces with an air of feigned reluctance; and his mother, charging him not to get before the guns, stands long in the doorway, under pretence of reiterating that charge, but really to admire the martial bearing of her husband, who knows she is looking at him, and wondering at the difference between a military coat and a farmer's frock.

The boy comes home with eyes larger than his father's; and the visions of that day fill all his dreams for the next year. He ventures out into the street alone; and with the first boys he meets he forms a military association. They march by sections, or in Indian file, as they call it, to the same district school. The schoolmistress makes them spell by platoons; and the boy that hits the target the oftenest in the eye she sends strutting home with a penny epaulette pinned to his shoulder. His exulting parents respond to this reward of merit, and give him a couple of India crackers or a copper. If the latter, a military fund is established, and the next day, at noon, goose-quills loaded with powder are shooting about the school-house floor. More extensive operations in the fascinating combustible succeed. A contribution is levied upon all fusible things in the cellar, kitchen, and garret; and the next week, when the first class of boys arise to read, every mother's son of them has a leaden plummet, a pewter button, or the handle of a pewter mug in his pocket for some patriotic object. After many mysterious givings out and giving in, a pewter cannon is added to the defences of the country; and then comes the tug of war. On the next Fourth of July, our juvenile and honourable artillery company appear on the village green, and contend for the mastery of the village swivel; for then every village had a swivel as much as a minister. Submitting to a subordinate capacity, they are content to bring turf and bricks to be rammed down the little rusty ordnance, and rum and sugar from the store to charge their parents with; receiving in return the sweetened sediments of many glasses, to inspire them on to manly daring and seeming. On that great day of rum and powder, amid the revelry and wassail of those who swore terribly and staggered home patriotically drunk for the defence of their country, those young minds entered upon another degree of their military education.

—o–o—

A CHILD'S QUESTION.

THE discussion of the Oregon Question had assumed its most serious aspect, when a British ship, the "Earl of Eglinton," was driven ashore on the island of Nantucket, and six of her crew perished in the waves, in presence of hundreds of the islanders, notwithstanding the most desperate exertions to save them. Some of the leading merchants of the town were foremost in their efforts to rescue the drowning men from the terrible

surge. They vied with the whalemen in venturing into
the surf, each with a rope fastened around his body, by
which he had to be drawn ashore the moment he had
got a firm hold on one of the shipwrecked mariners.
Several of the English sailors were thus drawn almost
senseless upon the beach, where they were caught up in
the arms of strong men, and conveyed into the town.
Every door was opened and every fireside ready for their
reception; and warm clothes and warm sympathies, and
every comfort that kindness could dictate, were in profuse
requisition to make them at home. The details of the
disaster were rehearsed, and all the hair's-breadth escapes
of those on ship and shore. An eminent merchant, who
had perilled his life in the surf, in plucking from its
fierce eddy a struggling sailor, was relating the adventure
at his fireside, with his little daughter on his knee, when
the child looked up into the father's face, with its earnest
eyes full of tears, and asked, in all the simplicity of a
child's heart, "Why did the people work so hard to save
the British sailors, if they want to go to war and kill
them?" It was a word fitly spoken, and it passed
around from house to house and heart and heart, and
many were made thoughtful by that child's question.

—o—o—

MILITARY PROTECTION.

A VERY industrious, simple-hearted peasant owned a little garden patch, which, with his persevering industry, yielded himself and family the means of subsistence. His cabbages and other vegetables were in the midst of their luxuriant growth, when a trivial occurrence broke the peaceful monotony of his mind and filled it with restless solicitude. A roguish little rabbit had stolen into the enclosure, and finding the bean and pea leaves to his taste, nibbled his breakfast from them, day after day, without dreaming that they were cultivated for shorter-eared folk than he and his dove-eyed companions. So he bobbed about amid the delicious verdure of the unrestricted Eden, and daintily tasted of the choicest things that grew in it, cocking up his ears with delight when ensconced by some plant of peculiar relish. Rising earlier than either the sun or the peasant, his morning repasts were finished without interruption, and he had retired to ruminate in his hole in a neighbouring wall, long before the poor man appeared, to detect the continued depredations of a guest that cooked and counted without his host.

Annoyed at these surreptitious visits, which had destroyed nearly a shilling's worth of his vegetables, the

K

peasant determined upon summary measures. With that self-sacrificing spirit which is apt to distinguish the patriotism of the poor, he resolved to "repel this foreign invasion," and annihilate the cotton-coated intruder, cost what it might. To make the means commensurate with the end, he applied to a neighbouring 'squire for his whole force of hunters, horses, and hounds, to expel the marauder from his territory by force of arms. The 'squire, willing to give the simple man a proof of his prowess, ordered the horn to be sounded early on the following morning; and the peasant was aroused from his bed by a squadron of horsemen thundering around his cottage, with neighing of steeds and yelping of dogs chiming in with the tooting trumpets of the chase. At the summons of the squire, the simple rustic brought out all his provisions—his bread, beef, beer, and hams—to breakfast the hungry host. And when all his stock had been consumed, the charge was sounded. The foaming and fretting steeds fell into line; "the dogs of war" were loosed; the watchword was given; the whole squadron came sweeping down through the garden, and the next moment every green plant and shrub it contained was trodden into the earth. The rabbit from his hole in the wall, and the peasant from the door of his cot, looked out upon the scene of desolation with astonishment and chagrin. The 'squire and his train disappeared, leaving the impoverished swain to ruminate upon "the costs of war," and the value of "military protection." The experience of every people that have enjoyed a " military protection " may find an illustration in the experience of this poor peasant.

—◦—◦—

OLD ENGLAND'S PLYMOUTH.

I CROSSED from Havre to Southampton on my return from France, and, after a pleasant visit with friends in that town, proceeded into the West of England, as far as old Plymouth, where I stayed a week at this old "homestead" of all the Plymouths of the New World, feeling attracted to it by sentiments of reverence and affection which every New Englander will understand. I was welcomed to its beautiful and cultivated homes with a grandfatherly cordiality, which made me feel that I was in the house of our Plymouth's mother—a brave old English mansion, all of the olden time—surrounded by scores of bland-faced uncles, and a host of cousins with the true English rose in their cheeks, blooming perennially, 'mid fog, rain, and sunshine, winter and summer, and with speaking eyes of merry light, all pressing around me, to fill the measure of my welcome as a transatlantic kinsman, with every friendly greeting to which kindness could give expression. Brave old town ! Its quaint churches, with their silvery bells, were old and grey; and a series of generations had worshipped in them, had been

baptized, married, and buried in them ; and the ivy green
had webbed their turrets with its creeping tendrils, and
hung the sunny sides of their grey walls with its thick-
woven curtain; and daws and rooks of aristocratic lineage
had held their noisy conclave in the towers for centuries before the "Mayflower" weighed her anchor for
the Western World.   Brave old chronometers, these still,
grey churches, with their queer windows looking out
upon the modern world from beneath their ivy eye-
lashes !   And there is a music in their bells unlike the
combination of any sounds that can be made by all
the metals of a new world.   Brave bells !   They do not
ring ; they sing, as if by inspiration, like a choir of
silver-throated birds in a thicket.   And they sung of a
Sabbath morning as cheerily as now, when there was not
a white man in America !   Think of that !   And they
are singing on, just as if America had never been discovered, nor any special accident had happened to
mankind since they first began to sing.   Think of that !
And of a Sabbath morning their music brings to the
courts which the old crusaders trod, children as young
as American children of the same age.

—◦—◦—

LETTERS TO AN APPRENTICE.

AS a little earnest of my desire to assist you, let me come and spend an hour with you every Saturday night in your cosy little room. When the labours of the week are closed, and you have completed your preparations for the sabbath, imagine that the "Letter to an Apprentice," which you will find on your table, is myself in person; that I have come to you not only as a teacher, but a friend and companion; not to solemnize your mind and check your buoyant thoughts with austere precepts and dogmatical rules, but to enlist the vivacity of your spirits in pleasant conversation upon subjects of attractive interest and cheerful aspect. Let me come to speak of what others have done, and you may do, to be wise, happy, and useful in this life, and that other sphere of existence, to prepare for the employments of which is the grand object of human education; to set up some guide marks along the road that is conducting you into the untested realities of the future.

I hope these interviews—in spirit, if not in person—will not only be entertaining, but instructive. One hour a week you may deem insufficient for many lessons in any branch of information. It is so, indeed, of itself; but, if the conversation of that hour should set your mind a-thinking for a whole week, that little fragment of time would assume a vast importance and value. For I conceive that not only one hour a day or week, but all time, and all the objects of sense, and all the necessities of labour and motives to action are exclusively designed to educate the mind into an everlasting activity and capacity for acquisition, which shall fit it to do, in a future state, what angels are doing now, and what they shall do hereafter in their progress to higher attainment.

I will not tell you now, into what fields of thought and study I intend to introduce you during the coming year; for you might shrink at the prospect, from that fallacious quality of sense which makes small things look difficult in the distance.

Every young man in this country, and especially every apprentice, ought to be grateful for the auspicious influences that are thrown around him, to develop the best qualities of his nature, and inspire him on to high attainments in moral and intellectual excellence. From the present, hereafter, and for ever, it will cost every young man of New England more obstinate effort to be ignorant than wise. The Printing Press, if I may so say, is stereotyping the earth with legible thoughts, and sowing the air with beautiful ideas, until *to know is to breathe.*

It is another subject of gratulation with me, that, although born in Georgia, you are permitted to serve out your apprenticeship in New England, out of the presence of slavery. For I cannot conceive how it can be possible for a young man to acquire a practical education and virtuous habits within the influence of that institution, which associates degradation with personal labour, activity, and enterprise. There would never have been a New England nor a New England people on the globe, if labour had not been honourable as well as necessary and profitable, along the whole length of our "rockbound shore." And, as I intimated that it would be the most valuable result of our one-hour interviews, to suggest thoughts which should occupy your mind during the labours of the week, let me give you this lesson for your reflections until I visit you again.

The peace, prosperity, intelligence, and virtue of any country or community depend upon the necessity of labour, and the honour they attach to it. In this is also involved the proposition, that a natural sterility of soil and severity of climate, and the absence of all mines of gold and silver, are perpetual elements of wealth and enterprise.

When looking over the map of the world, or passing through the country, you will easily recognize the evidence of this, which is as true and apparent in the case of a single individual as a nation or community : you need not travel a mile for an illustration. Compare, for instance, the towns that lie along the fertile valley of the Connecticut with the villages that line the mountain streams in the interior, where the rugged sterility of the soil has created such an ingenious energy of character and enterprise. The valley of the Mohawk, contrasted with sections of less fertility, will present the same curious disparity in favour of that condition which imposes upon a community the necessity of laborious activity.

In my next, I shall try to show you that the providence of GOD has ordained something better than luck, to insure the reward of industrious application and a virtuous life.

—◦—◦—

MIND AND INSTINCT.

ALL kinds of animals have as many senses as man, and often in as high a degree of susceptibility; and consequently derive as much animal pleasure from their gratification. Their sense of sight, hearing, smelling, or feeling is, on an average, as keen as that of man. Now, it is a question with me whether, if they possessed a mind, it would add to their sensual enjoyment. If they had a reasoning mind, they would never have occasion for a single thought; they would have nothing for it to do. Their unthinking instinct would be worth to them a hundred minds; merely because they stand in no physical want of thought, having nothing to invent for their comfort. If it would gratify a lion's appetite better to have the kid killed and dressed by a scientific butcher, or served up *à-la-mode* by a French cook; or if the ox could not eat his supper till the corn he had trodden out was ground and made into cakes, then the faculty of thought would be physically indispensable to both. But their constitution, being so constructed as to conform precisely to the impulses of an unthinking instinct, therefore a substitution of thought for those impulses would probably occasion them as much physical suffering as I should experience were my mind suddenly displaced by an instinct. For, in both cases, there would be no physical conformity to the new condition of life and action.

Mere animal life, then, ranks next above the vegetable, and, like that, is made for man ; and this is its highest end. The instinct of the ox was given him to make him a better beast of burden and better beef, not to create some faint resemblance between him and an intelligent being. But man's physical nature, with all its organs, senses, and necessities, may be considered as merely an auxiliary to his mind. For, as not one of those organs may be exercised, nor one of those senses gratified, nor a physical necessity supplied without the co-operation of thought, the mind is consequently brought into a continual state of action by the necessities of our physical nature. You cannot lift your finger either waking or sleeping, or hear a sound, or smell a flower, or see an object, or exercise any organ of sense, without stirring the mind to thought. This physical necessity of mental activity is created, not only by a conformation of the human system to a reasoning mind, but equally so by a corresponding conformation of the external world to that system. The provision for the constant occupation of our reasoning faculties is so vitally incorporated with the necessities of our physical nature, that the earth is not permitted to produce anything that can sustain our animal life, which we have not first to secure, change, combine, and prepare into food, by some invention or artificial process. In this respect, our mental education resembles the system pursued by some of the ancient islanders of the Mediterranean. In order to teach their children the use of the bow and the art of war, they suspended their breakfast every morning from the bough of a tree, and made them shoot for it, well knowing that their hunger would sharpen their aim as well as their appetites. So a benevolent Providence, in order to impose upon us a similar necessity and motive of mental activity, has hung, not only our food, but the gratification of every sense, as it were, upon a tall tree, and taught our ideas to shoot for it—or, without the figure, to think for it. Everything that can satisfy our natural wants or the yearnings of sense, we are obliged to bring into communication with us by some invention or the manufacture of some artificial faculty.

—◦—◦—

THE MOTHER AND MOTIVES OF INVENTION.

IN my last letter I promised to show how " necessity is the mother of invention," or how our reasoning faculties were designed to be kept in a state of constant occupation and progressive development by the necessities of our physical nature, or by just such motives as were brought to bear upon the juvenile archers of the Mediterranean islands in being compelled to fast until they could bring down their breakfast from the top of a tree with their arrows. These physical necessities, perhaps, may be ranked among the lower classes of motives that impel the mind to constant activity; but they are the most steady and even in their operation upon our intellectual faculties. The stimulus of ambition or love may and often does act with greater force, propelling thought to higher or deeper reaches of conception. I hope you have read Longfellow, and will remember his beautiful and graphic description of " The Building of the Ship," which terminates with such a stirring apostrophe to our Ship of State, so often quoted in our patriotic literature and public speeches at political meetings. The master's apprentice shows the action of one of these higher forces upon his mind, in developing taste, conception, skill, and labour.　See how the poet describes this mental stimulus:

> "Ah, how skilful grows the hand
> That obeyeth Love's command!
> It is the heart, and nót the brain,
> That to the highest doth attain;
> And he who followeth Love's behest
> Far exceedeth all the rest!"

I have translated for you, from the German, Gessner's story of the conception and building of

THE FIRST SHIP.

Many sorrowful years had passed since that fearful night, when Mylon's house, on their little promontory, was separated far from the mainland by the raging flood; for the sea had swallowed up the plain that united them to the continent.　Upon a solitary island their dwelling stood, so far removed from the opposite shore, that, in the softest stillness of heaven and sea, they could not hear the loudest lowing of the herds from the distant coast.　Semira had long since buried her husband; and there, with her daughter, in sad solitude she lived, while no society sweetened their hours, save the birds of heaven and their little flocks.

Melida, in the meantime, was wont to sport with the young lambs in fascinating innocence; to build little arbours by the shore of the foaming sea; to weave into bowers the odorous shades: she was the guardian genius of the plants ; for all their suffering buds and blossoms she fostered with assiduous tenderness. She had also made a meandering channel for a little fountain, where it might drip from stone to stone, or rest in little pools ; and around the island she had planted a double row of fruitful trees, beneath whose shade she walked alone, beautiful as Venus on the Isle of Paphos. She had also made a little grot among the rocks by the sea-side, and hung it around with diversely tinted shells which the sportive waves had brought to the shore.

Among such innocent occupations her hours flowed by ; and she felt not that she was alone. Sixteen youthful years had thus passed away ; and now she began to feel her solitude. Mute and spiritless she walked, or often sat beneath her shady bowers, and thus discoursed with herself: "Why have the gods placed us here, so solitary? More unhappy than all other creatures, wherefore were we created, and why do we exist? O I feel it!—whence else this disquiet, but that I lack something which belongs to my being—something which I cannot name! Yes; I feel that I was not created for this solitude : something peculiar must have passed over us, which my mother conceals. I see it— there is ever a sad mystery brooding on her brow ; and when I inquire the reason, then tears come trembling into her eyes, which she restrains with pain. But I will trust in the wisdom of the overruling gods : I will not ask ; in silent reverence will I await my fate from their hands, obscure as is the mysterious cause of my solitude."

*　*　*　*　*　*　*　*　*

Often, in deep thought, she looked out upon the broad sea, and sighed : " O ye far, invisible floods ! tell me, O tell me ! is this little point, this island which ye surround, the only land ?   Are there not other shores, too far for my eye, which your waters lave ?   Alas ! my mother denies it ; but I suspect her silent grief.   Surely this is not the only land within your vast expanse ; for what is that yonder, which like a low, immoveable cloud, stretches forth in a long line over your extremest border ?   Perhaps my imagination deceived me ; but I even fancied that, in the deep stillness of the evening hour, I could hear the hum of distant voices.   What else can it be ?   True, it appears small ; but this comes from the distance alone.   O, I know it is so ; for the distant waves also seem small ; and our house appears small, when I view it from the farthest point of this island.   And if that *is* land like this, with flowers and fruit trees, then there must be beings there, for whose enjoyment these were made.   But perhaps they are other creatures than these which we have here ; perhaps no beings like me ; none that would better serve me, as my companions, than my sheep here.   But if it were—alas ! the thought makes me sad indeed—if that were a land inhabited by beings like me ; and if there were many of them, as there are many birds and many sheep on our island ; and if they could rejoice with each other, as the various birds rejoice, or as my sheep in social unity rejoice—O happy, happy beings! Leave me, leave me, too captivating thought! Bewildering thoughts! whither will ye lead me, to make me unhappy? O ye waves! when ye roll against yonder coast, then whisper to its inhabitants, that an unhappy maiden weeps on the shore of yonder island. Leave me, ye wandering thoughts! ye make me sad."

* * * * * * * * *

On the mainland, over against the island, there dwelt a youth of noble form. He might have been taken for one of the gods, as he walked forth upon the blooming lawn, or beneath the shady grove. Often had his father recounted to him, how, many years before, a great catastrophe had befallen the land. "You see that speck yonder in the sea?" said he, pointing with his hand towards the island (he was standing before his house which was hard upon the shore): "a long neck of land, like an outstretched arm, once ran far out into the sea. On the extremest end there dwelt a noble pair, Semira and Mylon. Bright flowers reached from our shore to their house, and numerous herds fed on either side of the long extended strip of land. Their greatest comfort and blessing was then an infant child, a wonder of grace and beauty. The women of the land came from far around, to see the beauty of the child, and bring it presents, and bless the mother; but it makes me shudder to think of the catastrophe. Once, at midnight, a fearful crash, as of a thousand thunderbolts, awoke from sleep the whole region around; the whole country trembled; the sea raged and overflowed its banks with a dreadful roar; the cry of fear and anguish was wafted through the midnight air. The night was dark, and none could discover the cause of the calamity. Quaking and full of terror, we found ourselves upon the fields in agonizing apprehension; but the dawn approached, and then we saw the extent of the desolation: the plain between here and yonder island had sunk beneath the flood; and when first the sun shone upon a calmer sea, we discovered yonder island; and one of us, to whom the gods had given a keener eye, believed he could see, in bright daylight, Mylon's house and the trees around it. Perhaps he and his wife are still living; perhaps Melida—for that was the name of the beautiful child—is, in her sorrowful solitude, the most beautiful maiden that mortal ever saw."

This history made a powerful impression upon the mind of the youth; and afterwards he walked out often upon the sea-shore, and pondered on the fate of the inhabitants of the distant isle. Once, in view of the foaming waves, soft slumber overtook him; then flew Amor to him, and, sitting by his side, fanned him with gentle wing, lest the noontide heat should wake him; and gave him a dream, in which he thought he saw the shore of the island, and a maiden adorned with every fascinating grace moving silently and slow beneath the deep green shade. Gracefully inclined, she passed along in heedless beauty; her soft hair flowed down in parted ringlets over her shoulders, as milk upon the white resplendent marble; there was a fascinating paleness in her lovely countenance, as of roses that languish on some youthful bosom; and an ardour of affection beamed in her large, blue eyes. Thus she walked along, nor heeded the soft winds that dallied with her hair, nor the fairest flowers that bowed in adulation at her feet and charmed her notice with the loveliest odours, nor the sweetest fruits, which, in all their variegated tints, nodded from the waving boughs. Thus she approached the sea-side; and, looking sorrowfully over the blue distance, she stretched out her white arms, and seemed to entreat for help. Then he thought how he swam over the sea, and hastened to her aid. Amor received him on the shady coast, and brought the fair one to his trembling arms. Cupids joyfully fluttered around in voluptuous sports, encircling them with flowery garlands, and perfumed them with rosy odours from their soft, fluttering wings. The dreamer's heart palpitated; his cheeks glowed; his arms beat the fluttering breeze; and then he awoke; but long lay he there in stupifying ecstasy. "Gods!" cried he, with trembling lips, "where am I?—How?—she is gone—she has flown from my arms! Alas! here I lie on the shore—yonder far is the island! A dream—a cheating dream—to make me unhappy!"

* * * * * * * * *

Now sat he often deep musing on the shore, and with labouring mind meditated long and in vain upon some invention ; for the art of trusting one's self to the floods in ships was not yet found. What should they do on foreign coasts, when, in every place where grass grew for their cattle—trees stood with wholesome fruits, and a clear fountain bubbled—they found all their wealth, and a superabundance for all their wants ?   Long had he pondered, planned, and rejected, when, looking out sorrowfully upon the sea, he saw, at some distance from the shore, something which the waves were driving towards him.   Joy and hope beamed suddenly in his sharp, observing eye.   It approached continually; and at last he distinguished the thick trunk of an uprooted oak, hollowed out by age, floating along, upon which a timid hare, pursued by some enemy on land, had saved itself by swimming, and now sat there securely in the hollow tree, a leafy bough bent over it, covering it with its shade ; and a gentle wind drove the trunk to the youth on shore.   Intoxicated with the new conception, he leaped for joy upon the beach.   He dragged the trunk upon the sandy shore, that at early morn he might set about a work which yet lay so immatured in his imagination.   Hope and doubt watched with him through the sleepless hours, till the breaking morn ; but then, provided with slight implements (for few were requisite in the happy simplicity of those times), he hastened to the shore.   "Often have I seen," said he, "that a bough

overarched with leaves, being blown from shore, glided
easily over the water, and a short time since, I saw a
butterfly in the pool near our house, which, fluttering
over it, lighted here and there upon a leaf, nor wet its
delicate feet. I will try it. Nature has already done
half of the work : I will hollow out so far the trunk that
I can sit comfortably within it." Thus he spoke, and
joyfully commenced his labour. "O thou," cried he,
"whoever thou art, gentle divinity ! who brought before
me that memorable vision, hear, O hear my request :
let my enterprise succeed."

    *   *   *   *   *   *   *   *   *

A few days had elapsed, when the trunk was excavated
and assumed the form of a boat. Then he dragged it
to where the shore enclosed a little portion of the sea,
and protected him from the waves. He pushed it into
the water ; and, placing himself in the middle of it, he
suffered himself to be driven along the shore, wherever
the gentle waves carried him, and observed the success
and errors of his labour. The waves bore him back upon
the shore ; and then he commenced his labour anew,
altered and tried it often. "Now," said he within
himself, "half of the work is done ; but what means have
I to direct my course according to my will? In this
way I venture upon the impulse of the winds and waves
alone. It were madness thus to attempt a voyage
towards the island in the open sea." A hundred plans
revolved in his mind, and as many were rejected. "But,"

thought he at last, "the swan and all the other birds that swim in the water, guide their course with broad, webbed feet: an animal has taught me how to float upon the trunk of a tree, so may an animal also instruct me how to shape my course according to my pleasure. What if *I* should make me feet of *wood*, broad, like those of swans, and guide them with my hands, one on each side of the hollow trunk!" Full of ecstasy at the thought, he hastened to cut a convenient piece of wood, which soon he fashioned into the shape of two oars; then he fixed them to his boat, and tried them long in vain; but he watched continually the movements of the water-birds' feet, which suggested to his mind many improvements in directing his vessel. For a long time he glided about in the little basin; but at last, growing more confident in his skill, he pushed out boldly into the open sea, and guided his boat safely back, and, full of joy, sprang again on shore.

"O sweet delight!" cried he, "now has the experiment succeeded to my wish; now with the earliest rays of the sun will I trust to the sea, if the morning winds are favourable; in my little vase of wood will I commit myself to the floods."

* * * * * * * * *

"How your unhappy desire disquiets me!" sighed Semira. "The gods deny it thee, because thou dost wish it against their will. They can create beings such as thou from every tree and every stone; but"——

"How! can they do this from every tree, from every stone?" interrupted the daughter with animation. "O ye gods! by the side of every stone and every tree will I present you offerings; the fairest fruits of every season will I offer you, with tireless entreaties: aye, I will"——

Melida suddenly started back. "Gods!" cried she, "what do I see?" and she stood mute and motionless as a sculptured pillar. The youth was standing by the threshold of their door, equally astonished. "Gods! 'tis she," he cried, "'tis she whom I saw in my dream!"

Semira, completely astounded and full of perturbation, looked around and arose from her seat. "Art thou one from Olympus, and wouldst thou visit us in our lonely dwelling? O, then, be gracious to us, and——but how! standest thou there on the threshold as astonished as ourselves? Come in: whoever thou art, thou art welcome to us." Thus she spoke; and the young man walked in, and thus addressed them: "O receive me kindly into your dwelling! I am not from Olympus: I have come to you in a wonderful way; and I entreat your favour and protection."

Melida, while they were thus conversing, stood motionless; but her eye was passing over the whole beautiful form of the youth. "O the gods have heard my wish!" cried she at last; "they have given me this beautifully formed being for my companion. Come nearer, come to my side, that I may feel thy hands and touch thy rose-tinted cheeks. But tell me: how did the gods create thee ? O how will I unceasingly praise them for the gracious deed ! Tell me—what wert thou at first ?—a tree ?—a stone ? " Thus she spoke, while she pressed the trembling hand of the youth to her beating bosom. "My beloved ! " sighed the young man, "if I may call thee so,"——"*Me !*" said Melida, "O call me always so ! 'tis delightful to my ears. Now, for the first time, am I happy ; for all my wishes are satisfied in thee. O how my heart palpitates for joy, and my hand trembles in thine ! "

"Gods ! " cried the youth, "how my bosom swells with joy ! Long have I loved thee above all other beings. O how my fearful voyage has been blessed ! how well my bold undertaking has rewarded me ! " Thus spake he, and pressed the maiden's hand to his lips.

"O beloved mother ! " said Melida, "how gracious are the gods, that they should create this fair being for my companion—so lovely ! See, mother, this beautiful creature is as large as I, not small as thou once found *me* among the roses."

" Let us refrain," said Semira, "from our astonishment. Sit down by my side ; and thou, young man, be welcome to us. Thou canst not have come to us with any evil design : relate to us whence thou art, and how thou didst reach our solitary abode. Something wonderful must have happened to thee."

Hand in hand, Melida and the youth sat down

together; and he began to tell them how a god had shown him, in a dream, the beautiful form of Melida— how he had loved her—how he was tormented with despair, because the wide sea separated them—how he finally had built a boat, and ventured out to sea upon the hollowed trunk of a tree with wooden feet, and, under the protection of the gods had landed on their shore.

They listened astonished to the wonderful narrative. "The gods," said Semira, "have put it into your mind to make the fearful voyage over the billows of the sea. Welcome here! And to the gods will I present offerings of thanksgiving; for they have freed my bosom of these heavy griefs."

"There is, then," said Melida, "another land beyond the sea, and other inhabitants. I have always suspected this, although my mother concealed it from me. But surely thou wilt not return in thy hollowed trunk to yonder shore. O remain with me, and be only and entirely mine! I could not bear that thou shouldst love any other companion than me. But tell me: thou appearest not wholly like myself; fine hair grows about thy chin, which I have not." "That comes," replied the youth, "from my being a *man*, and thou a *maiden.*" "A *man!*" said Melida, "'t is wonderful! And yet I could not love thee more, wert thou my very image. O how much my mother has concealed from me!"

Semira smiled, and bade her prepare the evening meal.

They went—for the youth would go also—to pluck the fairest fruits. But, in the midst of their repeated embraces and tender words, they forgot the fruits which they were seeking, and strayed away to where the boat lay by the shore. " See ! " said the youth, " See ! there lies the trunk which brought me over the waves to thy arms." Melida ran down to it with eager haste. " O wonderful invention ! " she cried ; " O daring adventure ! In such a thing as this, which is nothing in the sea, didst thou trust thyself to the flood, the sport of the waves, as is the flying leaf of the flower the sport of the gentlest wind ? And did love for me inspire thee with such daring courage ? O how shall I thank thee for thy love ? But tell me : what is that fastened to each side ? Surely those are the feet of wood, with which thou, like a swan, didst direct thy course. O welcome, thou hollow trunk of oak ! Welcome, thou stranger from a distant shore ! Lying there, despoiled of thy foliage as thou art, still thou art more beautiful to me than any other, though clad in the fairest verdure of the spring. Blessed be the place thou hast shaded ! Blessed be the ashes of him who planted thee ! But thee, my beloved,"—and a tear fell from her eye as she spoke—" O I adjure thee, by all the gods I adjure thee, leave me not ! Never mount again that hollow trunk, to leave this shore ! If thou dost, may the angered waves drive thee back to my arms."

" Beloved one ! " said he, kissing the tears from her

eyes, "how unjust is thy apprehension! May the first
billows engulf me in the abyss, at my first attempt
to leave thee! How could I, when all my happiness,
all my joy abide with thee? On this auspicious coast
will I build two altars: one to fair Venus and her
mighty son—for he planted in my bosom this quench-
less love and daring resolution ; the other shall be sacred
to the god of the sea, who protected me when mounted
upon the waves." *   *   *   *

Their posterity improved the art of navigation ; and
upon the shore of the island they built a populous city,
and called it Cythera, whose lofty towers and temples
cast their shadows far out into the sea.

—◦—◦—

THE ENTAILMENT AND DISSEMINATION
OF KNOWLEDGE.

THERE are no rights of primogeniture in the
intellectual world. A man may give his lands,
titles, and money to his eldest son, to be handed down
to his remote posterity by a rigid entailment ; but he
cannot dispose of his thoughts in this way ; these belong
to the world—to poor men's children—and all they are
worth may become the portion of every human mind.
For when the estate of some great intellect is settled,

there are no dividends made of the property ; it is given entire to every member of the human family who has a mind large enough to take it : every man on earth may have the whole of it, if he can grasp and hold it. For instance : the devout mind of the great Newton pushed on beyond a point never before weathered by human conception. From unclaimed continents of space and unexplored latitudes of thought, he brought back a world of knowledge—for whom ?—and how to be divided ? Was it to be a diffusive legacy to mankind, or parcelled out into eight hundred million shares, that each member of the great family might have a portion ? No ; the Omniscient Mind left not the disposition of this immortal property to the arbitration of Probate Courts and financial administrators, but gave it entire, principal and interest, not only to every living man on earth, but to every one who shall live upon it hereafter. It matters not, in this deed of gift, whether that individual can or will appropriate the legacy ; it lies at his own door, in reservation for him and all his posterity. On the other hand, had Newton possessed what Crœsus owned, he could not, at his death, have given his fellow-beings a farthing apiece.

But let me refer to the illustration of " The First Ship," which I adduced in my last letter, and which may serve to elucidate the idea which I am anxious to convey to your mind. In that story, you were introduced to a young man sitting on the beach, and gazing, in uneasy meditation, upon the expanse of waters that divided between him and a far-off island, whose shore he fancied was defined in the blue, misty belt which bounded his vision. That island, he had just been told, had been separated from the mainland by a midnight deluge sweeping away the neck of a peninsula, and leaving a broad sea between the habitation of two lonely beings and the rest of the world. One of these, the daughter, had been represented to him as an exceedingly beautiful girl at the time of the disaster; and all the generous sympathies of his nature were awakened in his bosom, as his mind dwelt day and night upon their situation. As yet, no boat had ever been constructed, no unfordable river crossed: the idea of navigation had not been conceived. The livelong day he walked up and down the beach, straining his eyes across the intervening flood, and fancied the desolate pair were doing the same, and praying and sighing for relief. Here, then, was a mind under the operation of some of the strongest motives and impulses which could be brought to bear upon it, to propel it to its utmost capacity of invention. And, what is as true as remarkable, Nature, or Providence, always co-operates with a mind in this situation, suggesting by some incident the basis of the leading idea to be carried out. Thus, while his mental faculties are intensely exercised in devising some way to overcome the watery waste, he sees an object riding on the waves toward the shore on which he stands. It approaches;

his heart beats with emotion at the sight of the trunk of
a large uprooted oak floating slowly to the beach.   He
might have seen a hundred before ; but they suggested
no special idea : the developing pressure of necessity
was not upon his mind, and consequently the occurrence
left no impression.   But now a world of thoughts and
startling conceptions is involved in the motion of the
approaching trunk.   It gradually nears the shore ; its
progress is accelerated by an upright branch covered
with foliage, which catches the breeze.   His eye is
kindling with the inception of a new idea—the next
moment that idea absorbs a thousand sudden, novel
thoughts ; and the invention is half developed in his
mind.   He sees a timid hare safely ensconced in the
hollow of the floating log, where it had found refuge
from some enemy on land.   The transition is easy and
instantaneous—he fancies himself already crossing the
Hellespont to the fair one that walks in her loneliness
and beauty on the distant shore.   The First Ship is on
the stocks—he has launched it, mastless and sailless, in
his mind.   The keel idea has been laid, and every
subsequent one is framed into it.

Intoxicated with the new conception, he drags the
trunk upon the beach.   He falls to work upon it, and
finishes what nature had suggested and begun, hollowing
out a place sufficiently large for his seat.   Then follows
a long train of doubtful experiments, founded upon the
simplest teachings of nature.   He stops to see the butter-

fly alight upon a leaf in the pellucid pool, and, spreading
its gaudy wings to the breeze, sail across, with its tiny
feet scarcely moistened, to the other side. The yellow-
winged mariner is his teacher; and he carries away with
him a principle to be incorporated in The First Ship.
He watches the majestic swan and all the water-birds;
he admires the grace and envies the capacity of their
motion. He closely observes the structure and movement of their webbed feet which propel them through
the water; he notices, with an interest full of instruction, the symmetry of their form, the delicate tournure of
their breasts, so adapted to the watery element as hardly
to stir its surface with a ripple while gliding by him. He
runs back to his rough skeleton of a canoe with new
models and principles partially defined in his mind.

He "cuts and tries" a hundred times, and at last
works out a pair of clumsy webbed feet of wood, to
propel and guide his bark over the water. He rounds
the bow of his canoe after the model of the breast of the
swan; he widens and deepens the excavation; he attaches his wooden feet to its sides; and, in a quiet cove,
he commits himself in it to the placid waters. To his
infinite delight, it swims like a thing of life; and dry
and safe he rides out from the shore. He overcomes
the tendency of the tide and breeze by plying, awkwardly
indeed, his wooden webbed feet. The moment of his
great conquest has come; the sea is vanquished; he
rides, a conqueror prouder than Alexander, over its blue

expanse. He reaches the far-off island shore with an emotion of triumph swelling in his bosom. Upon the beach, new-trodden by the being his imagination has loved, he drags the faithful bark that has borne him over the flood. He hastens to the lonely cottage of the widow, and his sudden presence fills their hearts with rapture. The loveliness of her daughter realizes the ideal of his dreams and rewards the invention of The First Ship.

Now, I have not recurred to this illustration merely to show that Necessity is the mother of Invention, or to describe that condition of mind most favourable for the development of its inventive capacity. The particular truth which I would deduce from it and impress upon your mind is this—that such is the provision for the entailment and dissemination of knowledge, that all that this young man did for himself he did for the world. It matters not what he hoped or gained for himself from his invention; he gave the entire idea of The First Ship, so far as it was developed in his mind, to every man who lived in his day or who lives in this. I say, the entire idea; for it was entirely embodied in his canoe, which served as a model to all who could imitate it. His neighbour could build one like it without stopping to analyse that idea, or to reduce it to its original elements. He could do it without being acquainted with a single stage in the process of thought—in the apposition of principles and observations which resulted in the invention. The young man had done all the thinking, all the inventing for him. He had transferred to him the whole value of his meditations by night and his observations by day. For him had he seized and applied the bright and sudden thoughts suggested by the floating trunk, its mainmast bough, its leafy canvass, and its timid mariner. For him had he watched the butterfly, as, in sportful mood, it alighted upon a leaf, and made the transit of the pool with its gilded wings thrown out against the breeze. For him had he sat hour by hour upon the beach, and gazed upon the water-birds gliding by, witnessed the cause and grace of their movements, and reflected upon the graceful proportions which fitted them to the element he was studying to overcome. For him had he carved a model from their webbed feet for the oars, and rounded the bow of his canoe to the tournure of the swan. But did he lose any of the advantages of his invention by imparting the secret to his neighbour? Did he part with the knowledge he gave to another? No; the fountain of knowledge is kept full by its outlet instead of its inlet, and the more of it a man gives away the more he has to keep and to give. Though millions light their lamps at mine, it will shine as bright to me as if no other were burning on earth.

Thus all the generations of men, from Adam down to the present, have laboured for you, not to fill your purse, but to store your mind with all the intellectual wealth accumulated from the earliest periods of the race. All

the faculties of modern science are employed in con-
densing the thoughts, observations, and experiments of
ages into a single idea, which your mind may easily
comprehend and appropriate. For instance, the revolution of the earth around the sun and on its axis is a
fact reduced to the comprehension and taught in the
earliest lessons of childhood. But think for a moment
of the history of that fact, and what it has cost the world
to establish it. How many millions, of different nations,
languages, and tongues, have wrought, with all the
vigour of their intellects, upon that truth! The chain
of reasoning, observation, and experiment, by which it
it was developed, traverses all the annals of mankind,
and takes up links of testimony beyond the Deluge.
Adam, and Methusaleh, and Noah stood at the further
end of that chain, and passed the light of their long
years of observation down the lines of time ; and patri-
archs, and princes, and philosophers kept up the
succession, and passed on the incipient idea from
generation to generation, burning brighter and brighter
with the inspiration of truth. And this costly idea,
which you have appropriated to your own mind without
an effort, without money and without price, exhausted
the wealth of mighty intellects. Pythagoras, Aristarchus,
and Copernicus drank the bitterest dregs of persecution
for it ; Kepler lived and died for it ; Galileo fell down
bound in Romish inquisitions for it.

When facts like this, which have cost the concentrated

efforts of the human intellect for centuries to establish, are now brought within the comprehension of the child, how can you, or any other young man, deem the acquisition of knowledge difficult or precarious? When the science of the world has adopted you as its heir, and left the goodly heritage at your door; when all Christendom is full of affluent, active minds that are labouring day and night to expand and enrich yours; and ten thousand engines are at work, to charge the very atmosphere that you breathe with their bright and costly thoughts, what need you but the disposition to accept and the ability to appropriate a world of intellectual wealth?

—o—o—

SELF HELPS AND PROVIDENTIAL HELPS.

IF we look into the history of distinguished men of any age, we shall find this to be a fact, whatever it may indicate: their minds were all subjected to the action of two classes of impulses—the inductive and propulsive, if you will admit that term. The difference in the action and effect of these two kinds of impulses is simply this: under the operation of the first, a man runs for a nominal prize, a fading garland; under the other, he runs for life: the one is induced; the other is propelled. The inductive impulses, then, are the first that operate upon the mind. They comprise the influences of

M

early education, of taste, and the common desire to
excel. The propulsive influences comprise the action
and effect of those providential circumstances—those
sudden and fortuitous exigencies—by which the mind is
energetically propelled to its extremest capacity, and
sustains an effort exceeding the ability of any voluntary
exertion. In the physical man, this capacity is called
the reserved strength of nature, examples of which are
found in the wonderful energy with which a delicate
mother sometimes dashes through the burning timbers
to the rescue of her slumbering infant, and in every
struggle for life. We call this the reserved strength of
our physical nature, a fund which we cannot spend at or
for pleasure, but which is laid up against some physical
necessity which some special providence must create.

Both these classes of impulses are illustrated in the
venerated character of Washington, whose very name
stirs the chords of every freeman's heart, and the heart
of every bondsman who hopes to be free. The first
determinating accident in the career of Washington was
the fact that he had an excellent mother. But her
mere physical maternity had but little to do with his
character: she was his teacher; and to that very
circumstance may be ascribed the nature of his early
tastes and habits. Her aim reached higher than the
frivolous ambition of making her son a bright boy; she
educated him for a man. She had no weak predilection
for brilliant parts; she aimed at a perfect whole. With

the magic of a mother's touch, which is a secret between her and heaven, she gave an exquisite symmetry to his moral and intellectual character.

At the age of fourteen George Washington could read and spell as well as most of the boys of his class. He had also acquired a fondness for arithmetic, and a useful habit of writing down all his sums and problems with much taste and care. During several years of study, he had acquired a taste for mathematics. That taste was a constant inductive influence, supplying sufficient stimulus to lead him on to a quite respectable attainment in the science.

Just at this point, a providential circumstance, an accidental exigency, which would have occurred if he had never studied arithmetic, came in to the aid of his taste, and gave him a powerful propelling impulse. He was born in a vast, unexplored region, which was fast being settled by men who could not take angles, bearings, and the measurements necessary to define their own estates. The man who could do this was a man of importance to such a society, and received nearly half the land he surveyed as the reward of his science. A compass and several pairs of dividers were immediately put into his hands. He was almost thrust into a new field of study, with an impetus of new interests, motives, and prospects. Hardly two years passed away before he brought home to his mother an accurate plot of the fields around the old school-house, with all their bearings, angles, and contents beautifully registered in his field-book.

Another providential circumstance at this juncture gave him another propulsive impetus. After he had learned to take an accurate survey of his mother's plantation, his brother Lawrence took him to Mount Vernon. Thither he carried his compass, and continued his surveys, merely to render himself familiar with the application of principles and the use of instruments. Just at this time, Lord Fairfax, an eccentric, generous man, had returned to Virginia to take possession of the immense tracts of wild lands he had inherited in the rich valleys of the Alleghany Mountains. Settlers were selecting the choicest portions of this great domain, without leave or license. He needed a surveyor without a moment's delay. The young Washington was introduced to him at the house of a relative; he saw his field-book, discovered his capacity, and intrusted him with this important enterprise when he was little more than sixteen years old. This enterprise seemed almost to have determined his career. It opened the door to every department of public service which he ever entered.

Now, the arrival of Lord Fairfax and his peculiar exigency were purely accidental or providential; and Washington's introduction to him was purely accidental; and they would have been mere insignificant accidents to him, and not have furnished the slightest impulse to his mind, if he had not plotted the field-book of the old school-house lot two years before. It mattered not how much Lord Fairfax wanted a surveyor, and how few there were to be had in the country; George Washington would never have got the appointment, if he had so distrusted Providence as not to have fitted himself previously to fill a situation which Providence could alone create. His previous acquirements, under the impulse of taste, the incitement of interest and ambition and his confidence in the help of Providence, induced the providential situation, which gave his mind an intensely propelling motive, and pushed it to a development which it could not have attained under the artificial stimulants of mere taste. So it was at every step of his career. Providence never opened to him a field of public service until he had fitted himself for that department, in anticipation that such a door would be opened to him. Let the extremity of his country have been what it might, he could never have received the office of corporal, unless he had complied with the requisitions of Providence, and qualified himself for that situation; with the inward assurance that it would be ready for him when he was ready to fill it.

Here we see the development of the human mind under a remarkable series of consecutive influences. In the first place, that mind, after several years of careful cultivation, acquires a taste for a particular pursuit. That taste becomes a constant inductive stimulus to certain intellectual faculties. When its powers have slowly determinated towards a certain direction, and reached a certain point of development, another impulse is added to the accumulating force of mere taste. A rich vista of brilliant prospects, interests, and motives, opens upon it, and supplies it with a new and powerful impetus. This point in the life of Washington was at the time when his mother bought him a compass, and the prospects of an accurate surveyor fired his young ambition. Under the action of these strong, co-operating influences, the mind reaches the furthest point of development it can attain by the mere induction of taste, interest, and ambition. Just at this juncture, a providential exigency, which would not have touched that mind except at that very point of its development, comes in to give it an irresistible self-propelling force, to call out the whole of that reserved strength which is common to every mind, and which cannot be unlocked to be squandered upon mere taste or an ambition to excel. Washington was brought under the action of this propelling influence at the age of sixteen, when Lord Fairfax looked at his field-book, saw there the accurate application of the principles of trigonometry, and in-trusted him with that great enterprise which forced into immediate action all the reserved strength of his intellect. The mind, under the intense action of these three powerful impulses, attains a capacity sufficient for some great exigency or providential situation. Taste, ambition, and necessity have jointly propelled it to this advanced point. But if the pressure of necessity is momentarily removed, the mind does not fall back ; it retains all the capacity it acquired under the combined impulse of those propelling influences. When Washington returned to Mount Vernon from his surveying expedition, he did not carry thither a jaded mind, although it had been subjected to the most intense exertion. The propelling process of development had not been a process of mental exhaustion, although the reserved strength of his intellect had been forced into action at every step. The incitements of taste, the impulses of ambition, and the stern exigencies of necessity had expanded his mind to a capacity sufficient to fill a providential situation. When he came out of that situation, he brought with him all the active capacity which he acquired in discharging its requisitions. With that very capacity he pushed against the door of Providence, and Providence opened it at his touch ; for, like the more extensive kingdom of heaven, Providence suffereth violence, and the violent take it by force.

Just at this juncture, another providential exigency occurs, a hundred times more important and imperious than the first. It is not now a Lord Fairfax who wants a surveyor to divide up his private estate ; it is his country that wants a man, no matter whom, provided he has the requisite integrity and ability, to go on a difficult mission to the Ohio, to interrogate and inspect the designs and movements of the French. They want a man of integrity and discretion; one who is acquainted with the intermediate country and its Indian inhabitants; one can who bring back an accurate and scientific description of his course and discoveries; who can take angles, observations, and trigonometrical measurements. Now, it so happens that not a man in Virginia, except George Washington, has ever carried a compass into that region, and acquired the experience that is required for such a tour. The mission is urgent; and probably Governor Dinwiddie deems it providential that such a competent young man as George Washington is ready for the trust. He starts upon the enterprise, which may be of immense importance to the colonies, to Great Britain, and to France. The influences of taste and the impulses of ambition have accumulated a new force; the yearnings and inspiration of patriotism combine with the intense exigencies of necessity, and all concentrate to expand his mind to a new capacity sufficient to fill this new providential situation. All the reserved strength of his intellect is forced into energetic action; and that very action generates a new and larger fund of reserved strength for another emergency. And that emergency speedily occurs: he himself induces its existence. Providence not only offers to him, but imposes upon him a new and infinitely more important situation. He has returned from his difficult mission; he has fathomed the policy of the French—detected the aim, extent, and direction of their aggressions. He has passed the practised eye of the scientific engineer over their fortifications. Sketched with all the nice and tasty precision exhibited in the field-book of the old school-house lot, he has unfolded to the Governor and Council an accurate description of the French fort—its form, size, construction, cannon, and barracks. He has even directed his men to count their canoes in the river. His journal is published, copied into all the newspapers of the colonies, republished in London under the auspices of the Crown, not because of its literary merits, but for the proofs it contains of the hostile acts and intentions of the French.

A force is immediately levied to repel the invaders: and who shall lead it through the wilderness to the banks of the Ohio? Who knows the direction, the distance, the position, and strength of the enemy, the access to their fortress, the proper points of attack, the nature of the ground, and the disposition of the Indians? There is but one man in Virginia that possesses this knowledge and capacity, and the Governor and Council say with a unanimous voice, that it is Major George Washington; and the results prove the justness of their conclusion. Providence now seemed not only to create the exigency for the man, but the man for the exigency. The colony deemed it providential that such a man was available for such an emergency. So it was at every term of his geometrical progression to the apex of his glory. Even

the proud, supercilious Braddock himself deemed it
providential that he had such a guide and companion on
his march; and the shattered remnant of his army
thought it was providential that they had such an
experienced leader as Col. Washington to bring them
off from that fatal field : and the whole country from
Maine to Georgia thought so too ; and every direction
and admonition he gave the impetuous British General,
assumed a kind of divinity; and they were remembered
and recited, until they have reached us by tradition.
Had that unfortunate day been less disastrous Washington
might never have led the Continental Army of the
American Revolution.

Thus a chain of remarkable providential events drew
him onward at every step of his career; but they would
not have helped him an inch if he had not reached up
and caught hold of the first link of that chain and
drawn down the rest.   Lord Fairfax would have wanted
and had a surveyor, if Washington had never seen a
compass ; the French would have erected their barracks
on the Ohio, if he had never surveyed among the
Alleghanies; the colonies would have sent a force to
repel the intruders, if he had not been previously chosen
for the mission to their commander.   Braddock would
have marched toward Fort du Quesne, had any other
officer than Washington led a prior expedition of the
colonial force.   These very events would have occurred,
had he never lived.   He did not create them; he

appropriated them to himself ; he "took them by violence ; " he complied with all the conditions of Providence, and found, as every man will find, that in keeping them there is great reward. True, there was a divinity that shaped his career ; and there is a divinity that shapes every man's career, who complies with the requisitions and trusts in the provisions of GoD's Providence. Upon these terms, let me say it with reverence, our Maker admits us to the right of suffrage in the divine legislation which is to govern our character and destiny. Upon this condition, He permits us to enact special provisions of providence in our own behalf. The man that cultivates his field, his heart, or his mind with industrious application, has made Providence his ally and helper. On the other hand, the man who entertains a niggardly suspicion of Providence—who confounds it with an austere, capricious, heathenish fate, and therefore buries his talent in the sand, and drops his seed upon the rock—that man has repealed all the provisions of Providence in his favour. As far as his prospects are concerned, he has sheathed the heavens with brass, cased his fields with iron, petrified the sky, and turned the sun into ice.

—◦—◦—

EASY ACQUISITION OF KNOWLEDGE.

A WORLD of knowledge has been prepared for the acquisition of every young man of this age and country. It is a legacy that received its first contributions beyond the Deluge, and, at every stage of its transmission, it has absorbed the wealth of mighty intellects. And this inheritance awaits your acceptance; its appropriation is rendered easy by facilities never equalled in any other period of the world. It is accessible without wading through a tedious medium of abstract learning; you have no new language to acquire in order to possess yourself of the treasure. Let us estimate partially this last advantage, for it is one that renders learning and knowledge synonymous; which would not be the case if you were obliged, for a long season, to learn before you could begin to know. Now it is very possible for a man to be an indefatigable student all the days of his life, and not come to the knowledge of any new truth for years. For instance, suppose, at your age, I had read the Bible through in the English language very attentively, and that the next year I had read it through in Latin, and the third in another language, until at the end of seventy years, I had read it in fifty different languages. It would have

cost me a long life of hard study, certainly, and I might
have been considered a man of learning, even if I had
read no other book : but could I pretend that all this
learning added anything essential to my stock of knowledge? If I spend my entire life in contemplating the
same set of facts through fifty differently tinted mediums,
should I arrive at any new truths? No; the knowledge
which I should thus gain would be confined to colour,
not substance.

The English language puts you in direct communication with all the facts of history, with every department
of science, and all the principles of philosophy. It
gives you an immediate access to all the literature and
learning of the world; to the great minds that have
enriched the annals of the race; to everything beautiful
or sublime in thought, word, or deed. You need not
wade through Latin or Greek to get at these treasures
of knowledge, for they have all been Anglicised to your
hand. Should you devote ten years of close study to
either or both of those languages, you would find a
field that had been reaped, and gleaned, and transferred
to that of your own native tongue. You may sit down to
Homer's "Iliad," on a winter's evening, without having
ever seen the Greek alphabet, and feast upon its lofty
conceptions, and get as near to the author's mind as if
he were an English poet. All that Virgil said or sung
you can read and comprehend in the evenings of one
week, without conjugating a Latin verb. Whereas, on

the other hand, to acquire the same knowledge of those immortal authors in their own language, would cost you three years of laborious study.

The field, then, is ready, and you can enter in at once. The primer in which you learned the English alphabet will unlock its treasures, and put you in possession of them. And, with a little economy, you will find time to enter that field ; for it is open morning, noon, and night. Let it be the resort of your leisure moments, those odd fragments of time that intervene between labour and repose.—*Letters to an Apprentice.*

THE SIMPLE CIRCULATION OF THE BIBLE.

THERE are certain great and holy instrumentalities, coming with such a revelation of divine authority and power from heaven and crowned with such manifestations of its favour, that multitudes of Christians feel that these alone are competent to sweep from the earth those great moral evils which have filled it with the most aggravated forms of sin and suffering. These instrumentalities, they believe, should absorb and employ the sympathies, prayers, hope, faith, and activities of all truly Christian men and women. These alone have the promise of GOD ; these alone He will bless to the highest well-being of mankind. And just at the present time,

the one which seems, in the estimation of many, to stand
in the very first place at the right hand of divine power in
its working upon the world, is. "The simple circulation
of the Bible." This alone will abolish slavery, war, and
the other great aggregate evils that degrade and oppress
mankind; and this it will do without the aid of societies
specifically organized to operate against these systems of
iniquity. From this standpoint they reach the conclusion by a single step, that such societies are unnecessary,
that they usurp even the prerogatives of the Christian
religion, and put forth the profane hand of Uzziah to
steady or propel the ark of GOD through the world.
Now we would, with sincere deference, invite those who
entertain these views to examine the foundation upon
which they base them. Can you find a warrant for them
in past experience? Upon what do you rest these
opinions? What have you read of the past, seen in the
present, or believed in the future, that inspires you with
confidence in these conclusions? Let us sit down
together, to examine their foundation for a few minutes.

Here are three great generic evils—Intemperance,
War, and Slavery We will not say that all the sinning
and suffering of the world are included in one or the
other of these systems ; but each of them, you will admit,
seems to number on its muster-roll most of the vices and
miseries that afflict society. Let us take, first, the habit
of Intemperance ; for this is fraught with more sin and
misery to mankind than both the other great evils put

together. War is a temporary tornado, sweeping over nations at wider intervals than in darker ages. Seldom more than two or three countries are smitten by its thunderbolts of ruin at the same time. The fiery tempest of malignities rages but for a season and within certain bounds. Thousands and tens of thousands of human lives are suddenly consumed by the quick cross-lightning of hatred and revenge. The storm passes over. The fierce elements of human passion subside from exhaustion. The sun, that looked with bloodshot eye upon the smoking desolations of the region, looks itself again, and beams on the land in its old way. The rains and dews fall, like the Samaritan's oil, into the wounds made by man in the face of nature, and blanch out the blood-stains with weeping water-drops from heaven.

Slavery, though it be "the sum of all villainies," is a system of atrocities inflicted upon hardly fifteen millions of the human family. Nine-tenths of the human beings involved directly in this evil are innocent of its existence. They are bought, beat, sold, and held as beasts of burden by a few millions of usurpers, who regard them as their property. Thus, if we may so say, sheer suffering predominates in the condition of slavery; suffering, not self-inflicted by the subjects of the system in gratifying their own passions and appetites, but put upon them by the cruelty and wickedness of a few of their fellow-beings possessing the power of oppression. Then it is an evil confined to limited and distant portions of the globe.

But Intemperance is an evil that lies like a miasma of sin and misery upon all the populations of Christendom, more or less dank and deadly. Steadily, with but thin and infrequent ingleamings or promise of pure sky and sun, it palls great communities day and night, summer and winter, year and century. No plummet ever sounded the depth, no line ever compassed the circumference, or traversed the diameter of the sea of crime and wretchedness fed and filled by the torrent streams of this black fountain of sin, hissing with the gurgling agonies of despair; streams welling out of the hidden desolations of human homes in every land; streams red with the ruin of immortal souls; streams choked in the yawning gorges of iniquity with the wrecks of hopes, character, reputation, once precious as immortality to millions of warm-beating hearts; streams dashing onward to the deep abyss with the maddest music of discord, in which intermingle and alternate the coarse ribaldry of midnight orgies, the sickly, whining wail of children pining for the bread that is drunk in gin, or hiding from the madness which it fires to frenzy in a father's eye; the yell of the maniac, chased and scourged by the furies of delirium tremens; the blasphemies of the Sunday pot-house; and the myriad-voiced murmurings of misery, in monotonous undertone, from fireless garrets, and hovels of poverty, and the sewers of vice, half hidden and half revealed in every town and village. The records of the prison, of the

N

poor-house, and mad-house, give but the facts that float on the sea of sin and misery which intemperance has filled with its fiery flood. And where is the fountain-head, where the sluice-gate of this bottomless gulf? Where is the beetling crag from which all these millions of every Christian land have plunged into the abyss at one leap? Not on the precipitate edge. Not one that ever perished in its depths ever reached it at one bound. Higher up, far higher up, among the greenest fields of life, where the stream flowed winsome and slow among the flowers, every human soul that ever sank in this sea took its first step to ruin. The custom of moderate drinking was the gateway to the gulf. No drunkard of any clime, or country, or age, ever reached it by any other passage. Custom! not any innate or instinctive thirst for inebriating drinks in the victims themselves at the beginning, but custom, the example of others; looking at "the wine when it is red" in another's hand; looking at it longingly when it is quaffed by a neighbour's lips, by a near friend, by a brother, by a father; custom, garlanded with the graces of hospitality, set all around with the brilliant refinements of social enjoyment; custom, consecrated by bishops, and Christian ministers of all denominations, by philanthropists, statesmen, and divines; custom, hidden by the Flood, "but seen on either side," continuous all the way to Adam in one direction, all the way to this morning's dawn, in the other; custom, set to music in palace and parlour;

set to smiles in eyes flashing with the fascination of female beauty; set to joy in songs of the select circle; set to literature in the first works of human genius; set to painting by artists half worshipped as divine; set to statuary by sculptors that have chiselled out heathen gods from stone that seemed to breathe a claim for reverence; set to poetry in the greatest epics in all times and languages; the rosy, winning custom of moderate drinking is the wicket-gate through which all the myriads that have been drowned in this dead sea of destruction first set their souls on the swift-rushing stream.

Go, search all the records of human experience, and see if you can find a single case of a human being that ever took a shorter cut to this gulf of ruin than this; that ever climbed up some other way, and leapt sheer over into the abyss at a bound. Ask the most experienced in the statistics of crime and misery, if he ever heard or read of man or woman who ever engulfed a human soul in the drunkard's fate through any other postern than this custom of moderate drinking. You have never read, we have never read of such a case.

Now, then, will "the simple circulation of the Bible" abolish this custom? Will the simple conversion and regeneration by the Spirit of GOD of the majority of the community abolish this custom? Will every person, on becoming a devout Christian, abandon this custom, and

totally cease to be a moderate drinker? In what
country in the world has the Bible freer and larger
circulation than in Scotland? In what country is it
more widely and devoutly read, and more persons able
to read it? In what country is the simple Gospel of
CHRIST preached with more purity and power? What
country is freer from heterodoxy, or can count at the
sacramental table more communicants, in proportion to
the population, than Scotland? Not one; upon the whole
face of the earth, not one. And yet in what country,
of the same number of inhabitants, are there drunk
such vast quantities of ardent spirits as in Scotland?
In what land more intoxication? The state and
statistics of inebriety in that highly-favoured country
have been recently pressed upon the notice of Parliament and of the public mind. According to one
respectable authority, "we learn that in forty cities
and towns in Scotland, every one hundred and forty-
nine of the population support a dram-shop, while it
requires nine hundred and eighty-one to keep a baker,
one thousand and sixty-seven to support a butcher,
and two thousand, two hundred and eighty-one to
sustain a bookseller." In no country is there exacted
a more strict observance of the sabbath than in
Scotland; yet, perhaps, in none, of the same size,
are there drunk more ardent spirits on that sacred
day; in none more intoxication and sabbath-breaking
concealed behind lowered shutters during the holy

hours. And the evil seems to grow, and even Government interference is invoked to check its progress.

What is the cause of all this? Is there no power to rise up and shut to the door through which such vast numbers are rushing into ruin, remediless and appalling? Why does not the simple circulation of the Bible achieve this? Because those who read its divine and holy precepts pretend they can find no positive prohibition there against the temperate use of ardent spirits. Why does not the simple preaching of the Gospel lift up a standard against this great iniquity that is flooding the land? Because the ablest ministers in the world cannot find a direct and fully-worded command against moderate drinking. Why does not every man and woman, on becoming really and truly a Christian, cease from supporting a custom fraught with such immeasurable ruin to millions? Because they see no precept enjoining upon them total abstinence from all that can intoxicate. And is it true? Is the Bible, with all its holy teachings; is the Bible, with an everlasting canon pointed against every thought and act of man's heart and every practice that worketh ill to his neighbour; is this great Bible, with its sublime and holy moralities, powerless against this fearful aggregate of sin and misery? No! a thousand times, no! Show us, then, the words: "Touch not, taste not, handle not anything that can intoxicate." These are not written in this categorical form of phraseology in the

Bible. We grant it. But within its blessed lids there
are teachings and precepts innumerable that convey all
the meaning and obligation of this injunction. Simple
teachings of the Gospel they are, and plain to the conscience of the Christian enlightened to comprehend the
compass and application of the command—" Thou
shalt love thy neighbour as thyself." And these are the
teachings and precepts which Temperance Societies are
organized to educe and array against this huge over-
spreading sin of intemperance, at the very head and
fountain of the evil—the custom of moderate drinking.

What is true in reference to intemperance, is equally
true in regard to slavery or war. The simple circulation
of the Bible, in the sense to which it is limited by those
who seem to oppose it to efforts of organized Christian
philanthropy, will no more abolish slavery or war than
it will intemperance.

In no part of America is the pure and simple Gospel
preached with such strong professions of orthodoxy as
in the slave States. In no part of the Union is there
comparatively so little of the Socinian leaven as in that
region of slaves. Yet these evangelical ministers cannot find a direct command within the pages of divine
revelation to utter in the slaveholder's ear—" Thou
shalt not hold thy fellow-being in bondage." Christian
ministers, in non-slaveholding states, concede they can
find no such command in the Old Testament or the
New. Nay, the Bible is searched with the keenest

acumen for precepts and precedents that sanction slavery; and a thousand teachers of the religion of JESUS, who took the humanity of the slave, and died equally for his salvation, insist that they cannot find this sanction.

So it is with War. The most Protestant country on the earth—a country which has circulated more Bibles, at home and in foreign lands, than any other on the globe—has waged more wars, during the last five hundred years, than any other nation in Christendom. Perhaps it is not too much to say, that nineteen out of every twenty Christian ministers in Great Britain sincerely believe that there is no precept in the Gospel of CHRIST that directly enjoins upon His followers a total abstinence from participation in any war, waged under any circumstances. And it is this fact that creates the necessity of special organized efforts to array the truths and teachings of Christianity against these mighty evils, which have been left almost untouched by what is called the simple circulation of the Bible, or the simple preaching of the Gospel.

—o—o—

EIGHTEEN HUNDRED AND FIFTY-TWO.

EIGHTEEN hundred and fifty-two! A great year has gone, with its illustrious events—not into the grave of time; for such events cannot die, or cease to act in the living experience of humanity. When a great and good man dies, many are tempted to say, in the first aspect and appreciation of the loss, "We shall not see his like again." Perhaps not, in the right line of succession of the deceased. For good and great men frequently leave no children behind them, or such as do not inherit their virtues. But a great year does not die in this way, childless and heirless. Such events as the Great Exhibition, the Peace Congress, the linking of London with all the great capitals of the continent by the submarine telegraph, and other illustrious trans-actions of 1851, are not enterprises that have breathed their last and been buried by the way-side of time during the travel and the endeavour of the last twelve months. No; they will live and breathe, be and do, in the living present and hopeful future of this generation and of others that are to come. A right glorious year has been this 1851, to which we have just bid adieu from the habit of our inverted ideas to think that humanity is rowing up stream to eternity, and that time is not a

tributary to that boundless ocean, but a river running
swiftly backward toward the beginning of the creation.
We know not how many of our readers remember 1801.
The few that do were young then; but the capital events
and expectations of that first year of the century must be
still fresh in their memories. They alone can contrast
these vividly with the doings of 1851. Without wishing
to be older than we are, we could almost wish ourselves
their experience, that we might better compare with each
other these two year-links in the chain of human progression—1801 and 1851! In what a contrast stand
before us the sire and son of the century! How grim,
shaggy, and barbarous the mien and mind of the former!
Look at its doings, plannings, and expectations, its
marches and counter-marches, its utmost and extremest
energies all converging toward the field of Waterloo.
Look at all the covert and overt agencies and influences
of hereditary jealousies and animosities which it set in
operation, to marshal upon that scene of carnage its
bloody congress of nations! How all its science and
genius wrought to this fierce encounter! Contrast this
with the Waterloo of 1851 in Hyde Park, with its
congress of nations in the Crystal Palace! Come now,
is there not a hopeful difference here? Has not the last
half, the son of the century, started off on its journey
with a pretty good outfit of prospect and promise? We
would put this to the sombre-eyed and timorous of faith,
who are looking for clouds in the horizon of the future.

It is a part of the blessing and value of a good man that when he has entered into his rest, his labours, his good works, follow him, not into the grave, like the wives of some eastern prince or the trinkets of an Indian savage, but follow—succeed him, walk and work after him, through time, for the well-being of humanity. Even so it is, and ever shall be with a good year. Chronologically it may cease and determinate as a duration. In the short-lived impressions of past existence it may sink like a dewdrop in the breaking gulf of time; and soon our memories may not "take it unmingled thence" into distinct appreciation. But the events it has begotten and borne on its bosom will not sink, nor float like the broken beams of a wrecked vision into eternity. No; its good works will follow it, in all the integrity and vigour of their influence. What a legacy this from the past and present to the future! What a manifest provision of divine Providence, to advance the enlightenment and well-being of mankind by a geometrical ratio of progression! How every step we take is multiplied into all the gradations of past progress! All the great and good deeds, all the agencies and influences that have been produced and producing for a hundred generations are the working capital with which 1852 enters upon its limited partnership with the past and future. Did ever a year, since the Christian era, receive from its immediate predecessor such a patrimony as the Great Exhibition, and the submarine telegraph, and all the stupendous

projects realized in the programme of 1851 ? The
twelve months of the year upon which we have entered,
with all its unrevealed experience, lie without, beyond
the veil which hides the future. The links in its chain
of events are twelve; and what the first will bring we
know not. It ought to be a great year to humanity.
It must be. It will be. Who can doubt it ? Let us
look to this future, to which we have come hopefully.
Let us address ourselves to act the part which devolves
upon us with faith, and full trust in Providence. Just
now, the semblance of a cloud may hang on the horizon
to which we turn our eyes; but distance under the
bluest sky looks cloudy often.

—◦—◦—

MANUFACTURING PUBLIC OPINION.

AS many of our readers are interested in that
extensive operation through the public press
on the continent of Europe, called the " Olive Leaf
Mission," they may be pleased with an incident from
which it originated. One winter's day, in 1844, we
were travelling in a railway carriage from Boston to
Lowell, Massachusetts, to attend a Peace Meeting, in
company with our friend, Amasa Walker, one of the
earliest and ablest advocates of the cause in America.
On the way, he related a little passage in his experience,

which was full of instruction, and made a deep and lasting impression on our own mind. He said, when he was a young man, living in Boston as a merchant's clerk, he was associated with a score of other young men, in similar situations, as a Sunday school teacher. Every Saturday night they held a teachers' meeting, for mutual enlightment in the lessons of religious instruction, which they were to impart the next day to the children under their charge. On one of these occasions, after the usual subject of their deliberations had been disposed of, their conversation fell upon a scene and source of demoralization which had long existed in Boston, without any remonstrance on the part of the public. For many years, the small dealers in ardent spirits had taken possession of the beautiful Common, a kind of park, which was esteemed the pride of the city. They set up liquor-stands under nearly all the trees that lined the walks of this pleasure ground, and each of these stands became the centre of attraction for a group of noisy topers; inasmuch that the better part of the population could derive no profit or pleasure from the park as a place of rest or recreation. The public mind had gradually acquiesced with the existence of this nuisance, until not a single voice was raised against it, from the pulpit, the press, or the people.

About half a dozen of these young Sunday school teachers, on the occasion referred to, remained behind, and directed their thoughts, with much sorrow of heart, upon this source of immorality. It was an old, inveterate practice, a kind of invested right; and what could half a dozen young clerks and apprentices do to abolish it against the sentiment of the public? Sure enough; what could they do! While they were dwelling half despondingly on this thought, up springs one of their number, with his eyes and face brimful of the light of a new idea. "Let us put it down," he exclaimed, with great earnestness; "let us put it down by the force of public opinion!" "Public opinion!" murmured his fellow-teachers, looking at him with surprise, and wondering whether he could be in earnest: "Where shall we get the public opinion to put it down with?"

"We will manufacture it ourselves," said the apprentice, with increased animation. His companions opened their eyes wider than before at this proposition; but the stare of incredulity was soon changed into a lively expression of faith, as the young man developed his idea, which was this: that their band of six should open a running fire of paragraphs, in the six daily journals of the city, against the nuisance, the very next week. With earnest unanimity they agreed to try the experiment. A., the author of the proposition, engaged to send a short article on the subject to the "Boston Atlas," early on the following Monday morning. B. agreed to send one to the "Boston Courier" on Tuesday. C. to the "Boston Post" on Wednesday, and so on through the week, until the six daily papers had been supplied each with a paragraph on the topic. They all went home full of this idea; and on Monday, sure enough, the " Boston Atlas " brings out a short, vigorous article against the nuisance of the liquor-stands on the Common, over the signature of A. The next day, a forcible paragraph appears in the "Courier," signed by B., expressing his complete and hearty concurrence with the views of the writer in the " Atlas," and urging the abolition of the crying evil with new arguments. On the following day, out comes the " Post " with an article in the same strain, written by some one who signed himself C. There was something remarkable in this, and people began to open their eyes to the subject. Thursday, Friday, and Saturday brought forth similar articles in the other three daily papers. It was astonishing. Here were six journals, some of them so antagonistically arrayed against each other on political questions, that they rarely would agree, even on a subject of common interest, now all uniting to demand the immediate and total abolition of the liquor-stands on the Common. Such a unanimous expression of public opinion had scarcely ever been heard of in Boston; and it became the common talk on 'Change by Saturday. The young men, who were circulating among the old merchants of the city at that place of meeting, frequently saw one taking the other by the button-hole, and heard him expressing his opinion somewhat after this fashion: " I am glad to find that the public mind has at last been aroused against this disgraceful nuisance. I have long regarded it a sin and a shame to the city to tolerate such an evil. For years our wives and daughters have not been able to walk or breathe with any comfort in our beautiful Common, because it was infested with gangs of noisy topers and smokers, swarming around the pernicious liquor-stands. I am glad, and the whole city ought to rejoice, that public opinion has at last arisen in its power to put down this shameful practice."

On that Saturday evening, the little band of Sunday school teachers came together with their hearts beating with the brightest expectations. After the usual exercises of their meeting had been brought to a close, they joyfully compared notes on the state of the popular mind in reference to the evil on the Common. And they came to the unanimous conclusion that a sufficient force of public opinion had already been manufactured to put down the nuisance. So it was agreed, that, on the following week, they should collect and concentrate this opinion in the form of a great petition, signed by the most influential men of the city. They, therefore, appointed a delegation to wait upon Harrison Gray Otis, the oldest patriarch and patriot of Boston, whose mansion overlooked the Common, and the scenes it daily presented, with the hope of securing his name to head the petition to the Town Council for the abolition of the evil. He received them with the greatest benignity, and said that he was happy to sign such a petition—that he had long regarded the shameful desecration of the Common as a source of great demoralization, and exceedingly detrimental to the best interests of the city, and he rejoiced that public opinion at last called for its entire abolition. More than a thousand of the first merchants and men of weight in Boston affixed their names to the petition, all expressing their satisfaction that the crying evil was to be put down by the force of public opinion. The petition, with its long array of influential signatures, was presented to the Town Council, and the liquor-stands were swept for ever from the beautiful Boston Common; and the city regards the achievement to this day as one of the triumphs of public opinion.

This interesting process of reaching and affecting the public mind was rich with suggestion, and we resolved to try the experiment in putting in circulation the doctrines of peace and human brotherhood. We therefore endeavoured to enlist a band of twenty-six paragraph writers, a number equal to that of the States in the American Union, each of whom would engage to write or prepare a short article or paragraph once a week, on the subject of peace, for some journal. We proposed that these twenty-six writers, whose initials would employ all the letters of the alphabet, should each take a State, and send a written paragraph to its leading journal. But to introduce into each of these journals a variety of style, and to make the presentation of these principles more impressive, we proposed that the twenty-six writers should follow each other in alphabetical order, through every one of the State journals selected as the medium of communication with the public mind; that is, A. would appear in the Massachusetts' journal one week, B. the next; followed, at weekly intervals, by all the initials of the alphabet. Thus, twenty-six writers would pass twice a year through every one of the twenty-six State journals. We were confident that if this system could be prosecuted for a year, a strong force of public opinion would be manufactured in favour of peace.

But there was one serious obstacle to the realization of this project which we could not overcome. It would have been possible to have found writers enough to produce twenty-six paragraphs a week; but the postage on half of them was a shilling, or twenty-five cents. This was a charge which we could not reasonably impose upon those who took the trouble to write these short articles. If we had at our command that mighty moral agency which the friends of peace in England enjoy, the penny post, we could have carried the plan into execution; but, cramped by this postal restriction, we were obliged to relinquish this cherished scheme, and resort to another, less expensive, and one which we could bring within the compass of our own personal exertions. We, therefore, tried an experiment with another little plan of operations, suggested by the

o

difficulties which the first encountered. We wrote a
short article, occupying the space of about a third of
a column of a common newspaper. This we had printed
on a small slip, headed by a dove with its token of peace,
and entitled, "An Olive Leaf for the People." By
issuing this periodically, it was admitted to the postal
rights of a newspaper, and could be sent to all the
journals of the United States without any charge at all.
With somewhat of doubtful expectation in reference to
the success of this experiment, we only ventured to send
out twelve copies of our first "Olive Leaf" to twelve of
those journals in New England which we thought most
favourably disposed to receive them. If three of these
would insert the articles, we felt that it would establish
the success of the operation. To our great encouragement, six of them did this very cordially. Next week,
we sent out the dove with twenty-five "Olive Leaves,"
with proportionate success. We were thus encouraged
to double our weekly editions, until we at last sent these
silent leaves of peace to a thousand newspapers, scattered
all over the American Union, two hundred of which, to
our personal knowledge, inserted them conspicuously as
selected articles. We also sent them to the British
provinces; and we recollect, with great pleasure, that
one morning we found on our table a journal from
Halifax, Nova Scotia, and one from Lexington, in Mis-
souri, almost within the shadow of the Rocky Mountains,
both containing the same "Olive Leaf," though nearly

three thousand miles of space separated the places of publication. We also sent a copy to every member of the United States Congress, of both Houses, which could be done without any charge for postage. The whole cost for printing and paper for fifteen hundred "Olive Leaves" did not exceed five dollars, or one pound; and we always folded, directed, and posted them ourself, so that no additional charge was incurred. The summer nights which we spent alone in this exercise in our "little upper room" of six stories' height, in the Exchange Buildings, Worcester, Massachusetts, are associated with most genial recollections, and assume new interest as we revert to them through the experience of these last great years of progress in the cause. We carried on this operation up to our leaving America for old England, in 1846. And although we are unable to say what influence it produced upon the community, yet we are encouraged to believe, that, through this cheap, quiet instrumentality, not a little public opinion was manufactured in favour of peace and human brotherhood.

Our only motive in thus adverting to the early and humble efforts which we have put forth in the promotion of this blessed cause, is to encourage especially the Olive Leaf Societies in Great Britain and America to undertake another department of quiet labour, another field of seed-sowing, which, we have the strongest confidence, will yield them a rich harvest. There are now about sixty of these societies in England and Scotland, and we hope the number will be raised at least to one hundred by the 1st of January, 1852. Through the " Olive Leaf Mission on the Continent of Europe," they are now sowing these principles of peace among the populations of France, Spain, Italy, Germany, Denmark, Sweden, and other countries. We trust, as new societies shall be added to the sister-band, that, under the life-giving dew of Heaven's blessing, we shall not only drop two seed-kernels where one falls now, but see two blades of peace spring up where one now peers above the ground.

But there is, also, a vast homefield to be sown and cultivated; and we would commend to the Olive Leaf Societies an agency for this purpose, which may be employed effectively, at an expense of time and money scarcely worthy of notice. It is an operation through the press, similar to the one we have described. They are now paying for the insertion of peace articles in about forty continental journals, and in seven different languages. These articles are almost equally necessary to the enlightenment of the public mind in Great Britain and America; and we are confident that most of the journals of these countries would insert them gratuitously, if properly solicited to do so. We have already published four of our " Olive Leaves for the Continent" in English, each containing nearly a dozen articles of different lengths, on almost every point and principle involved in the subject of peace. Among them may be found pieces and paragraphs from fifty to a hundred lines in length, from the pens of the ablest writers on the subject—from Chalmers, Robert Hall, Dr. Payson, Dymond, Cobden, Charles Sumner, Dr. Channing, and others. Now, then, we would earnestly invite every Olive Leaf Circle, among other home operations, to take in charge the newspaper press of its own locality, and ply it regularly every week with short articles and paragraphs taken from the " Olive Leaves for the Continent," or from other sources. This operation will cost but a few minutes and a few penny postage stamps per week. We would suggest that only one article or paragraph should be sent to an editor at once, and that it should not exceed fifty lines in length. Let it be already prepared for the hands of the type-setter, so as not to give the editor the trouble of making a single mark upon it with his pen. It should always be accompanied with a note, asking him, in a few words of respectful confidence, to insert it as a token of his good-will for the cause. Many excellent passages may be found in the works of distinguished writers who have touched incidentally on the subject, such as Sir James Macintosh, Dr. Johnson, Dr. Arnold, Macaulay, and others.

Now, if the Olive Leaf Societies will but lend a hand to this work, they may easily ply all the newspapers in Great Britain, and Ireland too, with these paragraphs of peace. Let us remember the experiment of the apprentice boys of Boston, and see if our efforts will not be crowned with their success in MANUFACTURING PUBLIC OPINION.

—o—o—

A WORD ABOUT THE WAR-SHIP IN BOSTON HARBOUR.

YES! there it is yet! that huge, lazy leviathan, with a hook in its jaws, tethered out to float and rot within the ignoble sweep of a chain cable! Great, pampered bully! swaying and swaggering about in this beautiful harbour year after year, when so many canvas-winged things are hard at work, like so many bees, bringing honey from every sea. Off with you, indolent old drone! Borrow a pair of wings, if you have none of your own, and be off. Your room is better than your company, and is wanted for mud-scows and other better guests. Arn't you ashamed, you pursy old cormorant, to be living on poor people's earnings at this rate? Why, you are worse than Sinbad's giant, before he had his eyes burnt out with a gridiron: his appetite was not half as expensive as yours; for it costs the labour of two thousand honest men a day to keep you in lounging order. Uncle Sam, have you nothing for this big ship to do? Set it about something: it takes up too much room here. Come, these Boston folks will give it a job that will set all its lazy hands at work to some profit to the country. They want a thousand ship-loads of gravel to build new wharves with, and your lubberly ship here is just the thing for it. Up with your anchor, and be off! It is the best freight it will ever get. Come, bid it spread its huge wings once, and see if it can fly. Send it to some foreign shore for a load of mules, guano, or sheepskins; or let it go a-whaling, cod-fishing, or after mackerel, or follow any honourable and useful vocation. Throw overboard that black, savage freight of granulated sulphur and cast-iron, and ship a thousand hoes, harpoons, hand-saws, or any implements of honest labour, and set those able and costly hands at work.

Uncle Sam! are those your boys swarming out like bees upon that forest of bare poles—unsuspendered, check-shirted boys? It is a bad way in which you are bringing them up, in the sight of this busy, working world. We can't afford, sir, to have our boys used up in this fashion. This is a great country; and they are wanted to hoe corn, dig potatoes, and go to mill and to the district school, and fill other honourable professions. Send to Africa, and ship a crew of light-footed apes that can skip from yard to yard, or bask on your fore, main, or mizzen tops; and we will risk the country. To be serious, old fellow, you are making us pay too much insurance upon this *terra firma;* and we can't stand it much longer. Why, just look at it for a moment. Take your slate and pencil, and foot up the bills of cost you

have made poor people pay for defences for a few years
past. There, you see, don't you? that all that has been
earned by all the merchant ships, mud-scows, and
schooners of the United States, for the last ten years,
would not pay the bill of your bullying, swaggering navy,
during the same time. Uncle Sam, do be a man of common sense, now, and listen to reason. If, instead of
defence, you will take all your cannons and muskets, and
make a Virginia fence of them around your new lands,
and row all your war-ships up Salt River, the brokers of
this old federal city will insure the safety of all this
American country and commerce for a million dollars a
year, and make a profit at that. Oh! you do defend
this country with a vengeance, Uncle Sam! It is the
sober truth, sir: this single war-ship, ever since it
began to swing around its anchor in Boston harbour,
has cost more money than the whole sum appropriated
to the religious and intellectual education of the city
during the same period. Think of that, sir! and every
dollar of it has been coined out of the sweat of honest
labour. Men that wield crow-bars, hoes, hammers, and
harpoons have to foot this bill; for all the guns and long
butcher-knives that have been used since Cain beat his
brother's brains out, never earned enough to pay for a
charge of powder and shot, over and above the cost of
loading and wielding them.

—◦—◦—

A WORD TO THE BOYS ABOUT WAR.

BOYS, did you - ever think that this great world, with all its wealth and woe; with all its mines and mountains, oceans, seas and rivers; with all its shipping, its steamboats, railroads, and magnetic telegraphs; with all its millions of darkly groping men, and all the science and progress of ages, will soon be given over into the hands of the boys of the present age? boys like you, assembled in school-rooms, or playing without them, on both sides of the Atlantic? Believe it; and look abroad upon your inheritance, and get ready to enter upon its possession. The kings, presidents, governors, statesmen, philosophers, ministers, teachers, men of the future, are all boys, whose feet, like yours, cannot reach the floor when seated on the benches upon which they are learning to master the monosyllables of their respective languages. Now, then, what are you going to do with your inheritance, when you come of age? Are you going to follow in the footsteps of your forefathers, and squander this inheritance, and try to beggar the world as they did? No, I know you will not. You will be men. Put your foot down there, and stand strong in that determination. You will be men, and men shall be the people, and upon the shoulders of the people—under GOD—shall be the government of this earth. Stand strong on this rock, in the majesty and might of this liberty in which the FATHER of men has set His children free. What next will you not do? You will not set up or worship any human gods, and pour out your blood and treasure in vain oblations to ideal deities, as all your predecessors have done.

You will not be idolatrous—GOD says you must not. We have recently been gauging the dead sea of blood, of Christian blood, most of it, which has been shed on the altar of National Glory.

We have been measuring the length of that row of human bodies which have been sacrificed upon this altar. They were the bodies of the people, and their veins supplied the sea of blood which has dyed the robes and sated the thirst of the red Babylon of National Glory, whose worship, in the softer appellations of genteel civilization, is patriotism. Remember, you are the people, and that GOD has said: "Thou shalt have no other gods before me." Do you intend to keep that commandment? Then do not worship Rags. The reign of Rags has been a reign of terror, a reign of tyranny for the people from time immemorial. You have read how the ancient Egyptians were wont to deify cats, calves, dogs, lizards, and all kinds of quadrupeds, reptiles, and birds. But all their worship of these squalling, bleating, screeching, creeping deities was nothing to the modern idolatry of Rags—Rags of silk tied to the upper ends of long painted poles, and streaming in the air to the sound of strained sheepskin and fluted tubes of noisy wood; Rags starred and striped; Rags with most of the beasts and birds of the Egyptian worship embroidered or embossed in gold upon them. Now, boys, remember that you are the people, who are to rule the rulers and govern the governments of the coming age. Therefore, hold up your heads like men, and tell the world, to all its continents, that they shall not worship Rags, however costly and glittering may be the silken folds they trail upon the winds.

There are millions of breadless, houseless, dejected, hopeless sons of labour, sons of the people, throughout Christendom, who have worshipped Rags of various bestial emblems, until they would fain share the crumbs with the dogs of the rich, whom their Rag-worship has made their masters. Poor people! poor people! had there been no moral distinction in the service, how much cheaper would it have been to have worshipped GOD and served humanity, than to have worshipped Rags which Governments have trailed in the air! Leaving out the blood, the deluge of crime and misery, the moral, social, and physical degradation, which have come upon the people as the reward of this idolatry, let us look into the ledger of the Christian world, and see what this Rag-worship has cost the people in money, money extorted from their hard-toiling hands; in bread taken from the mouths of their hungry children; in clothes that would have kept them warm. Well, here it is. I have added it up carefully; I mean that part of the whole amount which the people have not yet paid for their National Rag-worship; the debts of the Christian nations of Europe, which are all the fruits of War. Remember, I do not add in a farthing of the sum that has been paid for the last three centuries of National Glory. The debts of the Christian nations of Europe amount to the nice little sum of 10,306,000,000 dollars, the arrears due from the people for Rag-worship.

Now the boys of Europe, the people of the coming age, will have to work out, at day's labour, every farthing of this sum. For kings, presidents, governors, representatives, never pay nor fight. These vulgar duties are left to the people. As the people will be obliged to work out every cent of the immense sum I have mentioned, how many days' work at fifty cents a day, must be performed to pay these debts of Europe, which are merely the arrearages of Rag-worship?

—◦—◦—

INCIDENTS AND OBSERVATIONS IN
THE SOUTH.

BEFORE leaving Wilmington, we witnessed a spectacle which we would not have voluntarily looked upon. In walking up the main street, we saw a pretty large collection of people assembled in the most conspicuous place, by the market-house, and heard the auctioneer's voice vociferating with great rapidity, "Just a-going for nine hundred and eighty-five dollars. Going! going!—nobody say any more?—going!" We mechanically turned from the side-walk to the crowd, to see what was going for such an unusual sum. It certainly could not be a carriage and pair of horses, was our first thought: it might possibly be a house-lot in the city. "Going!" repeated the auctioneer; "Will no one say more than nine hundred and eighty-five dollars?" · We looked around for the article and the bidder in vain for a moment. "Going!" said the man with the hammer, leaning a little forward, as if to give the impending blow additional force; "Have you all done?" At that moment, the whole truth of the transaction burst upon us. We had noticed a negro man somewhat elevated in the midst, but thought he had been an attendant, or keeper of the property at auction; that his part was to hold the horse or cow for sale, and not the chattel itself. "Going !" His arms were folded across his breast, and his eyes turned under the brim of his coarse, palm hat, with a slow, leering look around upon the crowd. It was all the revelation of a moment; and a cold shudder thrilled our veins, like the touch of ice; but before we could turn away from the scene, the hammer fell, with "Gone to Mr. M'P——, for nine hundred and eighty-five dollars !" We walked away with our face to the ground, wondering if this strange transaction, that had passed like a vision before us, could, in very deed, be a reality. "Going !—going !—gone !" and that leering look of the slave towards his new master will remain in our memory as long as it clings to any incident of the past.

At nine the same morning, we left Wilmington for Charleston, South Carolina, travelling all night and until three p.m. the following day before we reached that city. About midnight we reached the Great Pedee River, which we crossed in large, flat boats — one for the passengers, the other for their luggage. It would be difficult to convey any idea of this performance and the scene connected with it. There was the deep, turbid river, rolling as swift as the Rhine between high, shelving banks covered with primeval forest trees of every foliage, deep, dark, and still. All was still and solemn and sullenly grand. From the railway down to the boats on which we had to cross this kind of Styx, fires of resinous pine branches were kindled at a few yards from each other. These were for general illumination of the whole space occupied in the embarkment. Then half-naked negroes, with a bundle of pine splints lighted in their hands, walked between the outer fires and the passengers down to the boats. To portray the scene revealed in the glare of these red, resinous bonfires and torchfires, would be wholly impossible. Up, and down, and across the river, spectral shadows and human figures, trees, stream and sky, stars above and stars below, mingled in a midnight vista quite indescribable. The slow-moving files of negroes descending with the baggage and mail-bags on their shoulders, the crossing and recrossing of the rude torches, and the silence with which the whole process was executed, presented a species of dreamy pantomime, in which the grand and grotesque figured in momentary alternation. The railway train, on the other side of the river, was elevated on a high, wooden staging, almost overhanging the water. To this we ascended by rude and primitive steps, partly natural and partly artificial, lighted by the pitch-pine torches. In the course of an hour we were again on our way, dashing through a wilderness of darkly wooded marsh lands, which cover a large portion of this part of the Southern States.

Towards morning we emerged into an arable region, and were soon among the cotton-fields, which, to ourself, were objects of new and peculiar interest. We soon made the acquaintance of a southern gentleman, who was very frank and affable, and entered into all the topics connected with southern agriculture and labour with great animation. He gave us many very interesting facts in reference to these matters. On passing the cotton-fields, we had been struck with a circumstance which appeared to us a little singular. In many cases the negroes were scattered about the field, each in a small section by himself, presenting a spectacle similar to that witnessed by the traveller in France, where a large field is often tilled by scores of half-acre proprietors. We noticed that every one of these slaves was striking out, with his hoe or mattock, with remarkable energy, as if he had a personal interest in every stroke. In other portions of the field stakes were also set up, as if to mark allotments. On asking the meaning of these landmarks, we were told that they designated tasks for the negroes; that it had been found a good policy to give them piece-work or a daily task to perform; that this system was coming to be extensively adopted, and was working well. He dwelt with a kind of enthusiasm upon the result of it in his own case. In the first place, it had entirely saved him the expense of an overseer on his plantation. He allotted out the labour upon it in tasks to his slaves, and he found they needed no bell to call them up in the morning. They would often go out to the cotton-field and wait there for the daylight, that they might not lose a moment in commencing their labour. Some would finish their tasks by eleven a.m., others at twelve, one, or two p.m. The rest of the day they had for themselves, which they employed in cultivating their patches of land, on which they produced vegetables of all kinds and sometimes cotton. This he bought of them, and paid always a little more for it than he received in market. This enabled them to gratify their taste for dress, &c. It was a great relief and convenience to himself; for he could go from home when he chose, and feel that matters would go right in his absence. It obviated the necessity of any flogging or scolding on his plantation.

To us it was almost amusing, as well as gratifying, to see the earnestness and enthusiasm with which he described these results of interested and partially requited labour. It seemed a great discovery to him, that his negroes, and those of his neighbours, could work without an overseer; could awake without his bell in the morning, and labour without the crack of his lash at noon, merely from the motive of a kind of indirect compensation for their toil, or the privilege of purchasing by it a few hours for themselves, not for rest, but for work of which all the reward was their own. Had some New England farmer discovered a guano deposit or a copper mine on his land, he would not have expatiated upon its advantages with more self-gratulation than did this Carolina planter upon the extraordinary impetus it communicates to the slave, to give him a personal interest in his own toil. When we parted, he seemed to manifest great pleasure that he had been able to reveal to us a new principle in the dynamics of human labour. Our readers will easily conceive with what gratification we listened to his fervid exposition of this principle.

We were deeply interested in seeing not only cotton-fields, but rice-fields, even in the immediate vicinity of Charleston, staked out in day-tasks for the slaves; as it showed that this important principle was coming to be recognized and adopted widely over the State.

AFTER-BATTLE AMENITIES.

WE lately noticed several rather extraordinary features of human disposition connected with the present most lamentable and cruel war. Different persons will consider these features under different aspects and interpretations; but it seems evident to our mind that they indicate new perceptions of the utter barbarism of any war that can be waged on earth; that even those bred to the military profession, who make war and its science, ideas, and practice, a business, are becoming more and more deeply impressed with its inhuman character; that they are coming to the fixed conviction that men engaged in the murderous conflict of the battle-field must for awhile lay aside their human natures, their reason, religion, and all the sentiments and

sympathies of a common humanity, and then endeavour
to mitigate as men the miseries they have inflicted upon
each other as lions, tigers, or hyenas. Especially has
this characteristic assumed a more striking and significant
aspect in connexion with the present war; in which both
parties, after the battle, seem to vie with each other in
acts of humanity to the wounded and prisoners that
have fallen into their hands, as a kind of sin-offering to
their own consciences, and to the conscience of the
world, for shocking both with the murderous barbarities
of the bloody conflict. It may then be regarded as a
very hopeful sign of progress, that the rank and file of
the soldiery of Europe are becoming more sensitive
to the moral conscience of the world, and to the dictates
of their own humanity; and that they do not hesitate to
express their horror at the deeds they are commanded
to perpetrate on the field of battle; whilst the officers,
being frequently men of education and high moral
sensibility, are furnishing us with many an instructive
testimony to the utter and inevitable barbarity of war.
We subjoin here that of a Russian officer upon this
point. A writer in a French journal, recently referring
to the Russian prisoners of war in the Ile d' Aix, states:
" We have made acquaintance with the Russian officers,
to whom we gave a very cordial reception. They
accepted an invitation, and came in full uniform.
During the whole evening the conversation was very
animated, and their information has enlightened us

upon many points which were before obscure or doubtful to us. We found no difficulty in talking on political questions, and had no fear either of wounding their feelings, or of having ours wounded by them. M. Furuhjdm, the civil governor of Bomarsund, who is an officer of the Imperial Guard, appeared much touched by our courtesy towards him. 'We are only machines of war,' he said to me; 'once off the field of battle, we have no longer enemies; we have only brothers, as every religion prescribes.'" How full and striking is this testimony to the dehumanizing character of war! The honest, simple sentiments of the common soldiers on this point are very affecting, and may be found daily in their letters to friends and relatives in England. One writes thus: "The same night, after the battle (Alma) was over, we formed up, and the roll was called; several were missing. That was a silent moment to hear who did not answer to their names. After we were dismissed to go where we liked, I thought I would take a view of a battle-field. We had run over the poor dead and wounded, but not to look all around. I took a stroll over the field of battle, and there saw above four thousand bleeding, groaning, and silent men, and most of them young men! That was a scene; and from all that lot I was spared. I bound up some of their wounds, Russians, English, and French." Another soldier gives us a glimpse of the after-scenery of the same battle in the following words: "I was dreadfully tired, for the band had to carry the wounded men to the rear, and assist the doctors to amputate and bind the wounds. I saw some dreadful sights that day—poor fellows' legs and arms off, shells bursting near them, setting their flesh on fire! the stench dreadful! We were up all night attending to the poor fellows, giving them water, changing their positions, and the night was awfully dark and cold, and being on the battle-field the smell from the dead bodies and the noise of the wounded horses was dreadful. I hope I never shall pass such a night again. The next morning I went over the plain to look at the dead, and saw the place covered with dead Russians—fine, able-bodied men. I went up to one poor wounded Russian, and gave him a drink. He was in great agony, and he made signs for me to cut his throat; of course I left him as he was."

—◦–◦—

ONE VOTE, AND ITS RESPONSIBILITY.

WE have seen an article going the rounds of the newspapers which was designed to illustrate the casual importance of a single vote. Instances were quoted where an important election was decided by the ballot of some obscure individual, whose suffrage was secured to the successful candidate by a winning smile of kindness or word of benignant courtesy, while threading his way through the crowd to the ballot-box.

If the article referred to proposed merely to show what a capacity of consequence might be given to a single vote by a possible concurrence of political accidents, and that without such a concurrence of accidents the responsibility and effect of that vote would be less significant; if it were to leave the impression upon the mind of the conscientious freeman, that the moral accountability and importance of his suffrage are to be determined by the parity, or disparity, or the critical balancings of the political parties, in reference to which he casts his vote; then, we conceive, the article alluded to comes far short of reaching the great fact involved in the case.

To the exercise of one's right of suffrage there inhere a moral character and obligation which cannot be enhanced by the emergency of a minority of one, or diminished by its estimated value in the majority of a million. It is not the difference between ninety-nine and one hundred that fixes the value of a single vote, or imposes upon one freeman a responsibility which the rest of the community may escape. His duty has nothing to do with the question, how many of his countrymen will vote with him or against him—whether his ballot will constitute a majority or be lost in a minority. He is not accountable for the adventitious importance or impotence which the action of others may give to his suffrage. Having discharged his duty according to the dictates of his own conscience, enlightened by studious and calm reflection, let him leave the consequences to the jurisdiction of Providence, to which they only belong. Whether in the majority or minority, is a consideration that adds no new obligation to his duty, which attaches no additional responsibility to its fearless and conscientious performance. Let not his hand tremble, nor his heart misgive, nor his faith be faint, when he approaches the ballot-box, through fear that some congruity or incongruity of circumstances may give to a single vote the power to change the destiny of political parties or the political character of the government. The case never occurred—it never can occur—where one man's vote has done, or can do, more in itself, than that of any other freeman, to affect a measure or policy in a representative government. Let us introduce an illustration that may make this fact more clear and instructive.

Suppose a delicate vase of porcelain to be placed under some " eaves of reeds," to be filled by the falling drops. The frail vessel will hold and sustain the pressure of a specific number, but will burst asunder at the weight of one super-added to that number. The vase is soon filled to its utmost capacity—a single dewdrop more will produce the catastrophe. The little, pearly globule trembles at the end of the incumbent reed : the next instant it glistens in the air, and the vase has burst into a hundred pieces. But did that last drop perpetrate all this mischief? No; every drop of the million which, collectively, exploded the vase, did as much, individually, mathematically, and philosophically, to bring about the disastrous result as the one that fell when the vessel could bear no more. But the vase would not have burst, had it not been for the weight of the last—the millionth drop? Neither would it have burst had it not been for the first, the tenth, the thousandth, or the nine hundred thousandth drop. The last—the casting drop would have possessed no determining force, if any one of the million had been wanting as it fell, or been displaced by its fall.

If this illustration is not in point, there is one in our political history of-terrible pertinence, which is not a dream nor a metaphor, but a fact of the saddest reality. Its analogies are not only the exponents, but the essential elements of the position we would demonstrate.

A little more than a quarter of a century ago, when this Republic was commanding the admiration of the world, for having established the principle that "All men are born free and equal," &c., our legislators were engaged in discussing and deciding the question, whether it would be good policy to reach up and thrust their profane hands within the palm of the ALMIGHTY, and fetter the unborn souls which He should breathe into flesh and blood within a certain section of this great country, called the Territory of Arkansas. After a great deal of debate, the question was taken, and seventy-three of these august seigniors said that all the human beings of a certain colour and condition, born in that territory after a certain date, should be slaves for ever, and their children, and their children's children, slaves for ever. On the other hand, seventy-five legislators said that all the beings of that class should be slaves but twenty-five years from their birth, and then be free for ever. This decision, that enslaved hardly half a man's life, and reduced the value of human flesh more than fifty per cent., aroused the cupidity of the slaveholders. A pretty market, indeed, would there be for slaves, if new slave States were to be subjected to such a restriction! Consequently, the next day a reconsideration was moved; and the question being taken, the vote stood: ayes, eighty-eight; noes, eighty-eight. And there they stood; and there the destiny of unborn thousands hung in oscillating suspense between the bottomless pit of slavery and the paradise of freedom. One vote was sufficient to sink them for ever in the one, or raise them to the full fruition of the other. That one vote was in the hands of Henry Clay, who sat in a chair above all the rest; and when he was asked to decide whether hopeless slavery should last for ever in Arkansas, he said, *"Aye!"* Thus fell his casting vote; and the one star of freedom fell from the bondman's firmament, ere its nearest ray of promise had time to reach his downcast eye. That irrevocable, impenitent, impenal, fatal *"Aye!"* it has long slumbered amid the silent things of the past—for twenty-five years it has slept with the voices of the dead. But this year it has awoke again, to thunder forth a new doom; to demand, with its trumpet tongue, a new and deeper vial of wrath to be poured out without mixture upon a portion of the human family. Yes, this is the year—remember it at the ballot-box, ye millions of American freemen—this is the year when every slave born in Arkansas in 1819 would have burst the bonds that fettered him to the condition of the brute, were it not for that one vote—that "*Aye!*"—big with perennial doom! This year, after a quarter of a century of latent inaction, it commences its terrible execution—it immolates its first annual hecatomb to slavery. Next year it will offer, at the same bloody shrine, a larger human sacrifice, increasing from year to year the number of its victims, until its slave-making potency shall be arrested by that Arm Almighty that shook old Egypt till she let her captives go.

Our imagination sickens at the scenes that might and will be enacted in consequence of that one vote. One has often moved before our mind's eye like a living, painful reality. It was in a day-dream that we saw Henry Clay, at the head of a long and illustrious procession, wending his way from the White House to the Capitol, there to take the Presidential oath and the reins of the Government. Between him and the great men of the nation, there marched in chains, and sad and tearful silence, three thousand human beings, whom his single vote re-fettered on the very threshold of freedom. The long cortege moved on; multitude upon multitude gathered around the Capitol Hill, and from every turret and pinnacle of our great Temple of Liberty, floated the nation's stars and stripes. The booming cannon and the shouts of the people announced that the President elect had sworn to support the Constitution, ordained to establish justice, freedom, and righteousness. And then a low, moaning wail went up from those manacled thousands, as if a new doom had sunk them deeper in slavery. We thought they were drawn up around the President's stand, chained two and two, their heads bowed to the ground like victims bound for slaughter; and at every eloquent period of the inaugural speech, they raised their pinioned hands, and shook their fetters to the fierce treble of the lash. And then the people shouted, and their exalted favourite went on, and uttered great swelling words about liberty, law, and patriotism, and all the other great interests of the Union; and pointed to the red stripes on the drapery that waved above, and to the red stripes cut by the scourge into the human flesh for sale below!—for sale, at his feet, under the very eaves of the Capitol!—flesh that his vote had made saleable and made a market for, till the end of time. And when he ceased, the great cannons spoke to the quaking heavens; and a hundred thousand tongues rent the air with joyous shoutings; and all the slave-pens in Washington sent up a tremulous wail of hopeless misery; and the American flag that sentineled their dungeon doors, unfurled its proudest folds and gracefully greeted the passing multitude, and beckoned to a well-filled warehouse of human flesh, and the slave-ship beating up for its cargo of enslaved humanity.

Did one vote do that dark deed? Yes; his vote did nothing less than decide that fearful question; nor did it do anything more than any other vote of the eighty-nine that were cast to make slavery perpetual. It required just eighty-nine votes to carry through the cruel act, and one was as decisive and, morally, as criminal as the other. There was not one of those eighty-nine legislators who might not say equally with Henry Clay—"My one vote decided the question in favour of slavery." If divine justice rewards an act according to its character and not its consequence, then upon the head of every one of those men rests the guilt of the transaction; and there it would rest if he had voted in the minority of one or the majority of a million. In either case, the moral character and responsibility of his vote would have been the same. Christian freemen! remember at the ballot-box, that no casting vote of another, nor the suffrage of an immense majority, will change one moral feature of your act, or diminish aught of its responsibility. GOD demands and humanity expects that you will do your duty in His fear and trust the result to His providence.

THE RELATIVE CAPACITIES OF NATIONS.

IT may be instructive and useful to glance at the present financial condition of the leading nations of Christendom, and to estimate their relative capacities of progress and prosperity. Especially at the present juncture of affairs, such a cursory investigation of the assets and liabilities of the principal Powers of the civilized world, must suggest to the American mind the immeasurable advantage of sustaining that policy of peace which was adopted at the outset, as a distinguishing characteristic of the Republic of the United States. In the palmiest year of European tranquillity and prosperity, they were far ahead of any nation in the Old World in relative wealth and power of progression. A two years' war, of unexampled waste and exhaustion, has vastly widened the distance by which the United States have advanced beyond the foremost European Powers in these comparative capacities. Happy and glorious will it be, if they have the wisdom and virtue to make these capacities work only for the well-being of the nation; for its unity, peace, and prosperity. Although such financial and commercial statistics as transpire to the public, from year to year, may not precisely measure, they, at least, suggest, the approximate wealth of nations.

But even in inferring their wealth from such statistics, no little caution is requisite, in order not to confound liabilities with assets, or indebtedness with sources of revenue. In estimating the property of an individual, it is pretty safe to go to the tax-book, and take the amount for which he is "rated." In his case, the amount of his taxes measures and represents his wealth. Even the sum that a man pays in interest on borrowed money may frequently and safely be assumed as representing part of his available means; for it should denote an amount of producing capital, so invested as to yield him a profit, after paying the stipulated rate of interest. But neither of these estimates would be correct when applied to the resources of nations. The amount of taxation does not represent the nation's wealth, but frequently, if not always, its poverty. The interest it annually pays on its debts does not indicate or even suggest an amount of money borrowed and invested reproductively. It generally stands for a sum borrowed and squandered upon an enterprise that yields not a farthing of revenue to the treasury. Take, for instance, the national debt of Great Britain, which amounted to 3,669,798,216 dollars before the commencement of the war with Russia. How little this almost immeasurable indebtedness represents of reproductive investment! We doubt if the Chancellor of the Exchequer could show that the investment which swallowed up these prodigious loans, yields him a sum equal to the tax he levies upon the single article of tea. With these observations, designed to qualify their valuation, we give a few statistics bearing upon the financial condition of the leading nations of Christendom in 1854, or before several of them became involved in the expenditures of the war with Russia.

Nations.	Total Debt.	Annual Charge of Debt.	Debt per Head.
	Dollars.	Dollars.	Dollars.
Great Britain	3,669,798,216	133,089,308	131.04
France	1,166,130,748	76,128,652	32.64
United States -	45,640,606	3,071,016	1.92
Austria	779,409,504	32,073,201	21.12
Russia	599,315,563	22,320,696	8.88
Prussia	156,867,240	7,804,041	9.12
Spain	695,217,926	NOT GIVEN	46.32
Sardinia	109,790,620	8,874,940	22.08
Portugal	91,789,440	3,163,238	26.16
Belgium	125,497,027	7,008,931	28.56
Bavaria	67,761,600	NOT GIVEN	14.40
Holland	480,395,337	14,483,793	142.80
Saxony	30,802,794	1,415,529	14.40
Denmark	64,999,996	2,314,790	34.08

From the foregoing table, it will be seen that the debt-burden of Holland is heavier upon its population, *per capita*, than that of any other nation, amounting to 142.80 dollars for every man, woman, and child. Next in proportionate weight is that of Great Britain, which is equal to 131.04 per head. The annual charge and interest of this debt are about 5 dollars *per capita* for the population of Great Britain, and 4.66 dollars for that of Holland. This represents the burden of the past and its expenditures, imposed upon the shoulders of every inhabitant of those kingdoms. Taking the average of the last five years, it will be found that more than half of the entire revenue of Great Britain goes for the past, in the shape of interest, leaving, of course, but half the financial capacity of the nation for the present and future. Undoubtedly England possesses more wealth than any other country in Christendom, and can sustain a larger amount of taxation. But this ability is not all available capacity for present or future exigencies or enterprises. The giant laden to half his strength may not take upon his shoulders another burden which a common man might not bear. Strong and broad-shouldered as he is, we must only estimate that portion of his strength which is not already taxed to its utmost, in measuring his ability with that of a smaller but less burdened competitor. Thus, in estimating the relative capacities of Great Britain and the United States, we see that the latter have husbanded almost their entire wealth and strength for present and prospective exigencies. The whole burden which the past imposes upon them only weighs, if we may so say, about two dollars per head, while that of England weighs 131 dollars. She is obliged to tax, annually, every man, woman, and child of her population to the amount of five dollars, for interest on her debt; while the United States have only to raise twelve and a half cents *per capita*, for interest. To make the comparison more easy of appreciation, let us assume that twelve and a half cents represent one pound avoirdupois. Then Great Britain has to carry in the race forty pounds per head, while the United States have only one to weigh upon their speed.

We have seen to what extent the resources of the principal nations of Christendom are mortgaged, as it were, to the past, or appropriated to the interest on their public debts. But these debts, vast as they are, do not represent all the burdens entailed by the past upon the present generation. They are nearly all the products and legacies of war, which, through the armed-peace system, imposes an additional load of great weight upon the people. In fact, the preparations for future wars cost several great nations nearly as much annually as they once expended in active conflict with hostile powers. Both these burdens are virtually the legacy of the past and its policy. It may be instructive to put them in the scale against all the other annual expenditures of different governments. We hope none of our readers will object to the classification of these two great items, if we call the interest on these public debts a charge for wars past, and the annual cost of military armaments and expenditure for wars prospective. All the other expenses are put under the head of "Civil Government." We subjoin these items, as they may be found in the returns for 1854. The amounts are first reduced to English currency, then to the American at the rate of 4.80 dollars to the pound sterling.

EXPENDITURES.

ENGLAND.

		Dollars.
Wars past		133,089,412
Wars prospective		117,984,201
Civil government		30,668,107
	Total	281,741,720

FRANCE.

Wars past		76,128,652
Wars prospective		85,152,033
Civil government		129,929,640
	Total	291,210,325

AUSTRIA.

Wars past		32,073,201
Wars prospective		53,744,596
Civil government		55,283,299
	Total	141,101,096

UNITED STATES.

Wars past		3,071,016
Wars prospective		22,501,822
Civil government		28,516,426
	Total	54,088,264

PRUSSIA.

Wars past		7,804,041
Wars prospective		20,184,508
Civil government		49,764,297
	Total	77,752,846

HOLLAND.

Wars past		14,483,793
Wars prospective		6,421,996
Civil government		7,375,694
	Total	28,281,483

The foregoing statistics show what a large proportion of the revenues of the leading nations is swallowed up in expenditures for war, past and prospective. These two items absorbed 251,073,613 dollars of the public income of Great Britain in 1854; while all the expenses involved in the civil government amounted to only 30,668,107 dollars. Thus the war system devours, even in time of peace, seven-eighths of the revenue of a nation that professes to be the most civilized and Christian in the world! These two heads of war expenditure cost France, in 1854, 161,280,685 dollars of its entire revenue, which was 291,210,325 dollars; Austria, 85,817,797 dollars out of 141,101,096 dollars; Prussia, 27,988,549 dollars out of 77,752,846 dollars; Holland, 20,905,789 dollars out of 28,281,483 dollars; United States, 25,572,838 dollars out of 54,088,264 dollars. Here are the six most commercial, wealthy, and enlightened nations of the earth spending, in one year, 572,639,271 dollars on wars past and prospective! As the ass in Scripture crouched between two burdens, so the people of Christendom are bowing to the earth beneath these two dead weights, saddled upon their shoulders by the war system. And, what seems to aggravate their misfortune, the burden grows heavier from year to year. With the exception of the United States, most of the nations of the world, instead of diminishing, seem to be increasing their public debts, and also their annual expenditures for military and

naval armaments. Nearly every year some new "improvements" in these arms and agencies are pressed
upon governments, the adoption of which involves an
additional outlay. Now steam must be applied to war-
ships, and a whole navy reconstructed or remodelled at
immense cost. Now the Minié rifle and Colt's revolver
must displace a hundred arsenals full of the old-fashioned
"shooting-irons," and saddle the people with a new bill
of expense. Now a ship of seven thousand tons,
carrying a Gibraltar armament of cannon, is launched,
and a great nation glories in its capacity to run over a
common seventy-four, as if it were a fishing-smack.
This is to be the *ne plus ultra* of naval power. Nothing
will ever go beyond this sea-giant of war. Before it has
made its trial-trip, the keel of a ship of twenty-two
thousand tons is laid, which, when constructed, would
run down the great "Napoleon" or the "Duke of
Wellington," as easily as either of them could sink a
common frigate. Thus it goes in the eager race for
naval or military superiority. The best paid science and
genius of the age are employed to stimulate the costly
competition, by inventing "improvements," or applying
"new principles." Where, when, and how is all this to
end? Is this ruinous policy to be pushed until all the
leading nations of Christendom shall break down under
its weight? It must work to this end, unless timely and
effective measures be adopted to arrest the evil. It is
proposed by one or more of the parties in the diplomatic

conference now sitting in Paris, that a great Peace
Congress of all the European governments shall be held,
to discuss and adjust the moot questions of that continent. No subject of more vital importance could come
before such a congress of nations than some practical
plan for putting an end to this ruinous armed-peace
system, which is dragging them into the abyss of bankruptcy. They have reached almost the brink of the
precipice by proportionate and simultaneous increase of
war armaments. The only way of escape is to retrace
their steps; that is, by proportionate and simultaneous
disarmament. In such a Congress, it should be as easy
to do this as to neutralize the Black Sea, or to limit
the number of war-ships in its waters. No nation of
Christendom would change its position, or lose any
of its relative strength by this arrangement. "If from
equals you take equals, the remainders will be equals,"
is clear enough; and it is equally clear, that if from
unequals you take equals, the original inequality will not
be affected by an iota either way. To reduce simultaneously the naval armaments of Christendom by so
many men per thousand, would leave all the nations in
the same relative force as at the present moment. Can
any intelligent and candid mind see any other way of
extricating those nations from the bog in which they are
floundering? Can any impartial man suggest an arrangement more important to their well-being than such a
disarmament? The only motive and object which the

United States should have in taking part in the proposed Congress, if invited, should be to press the adoption of this measure.

—◦—◦—

THE WASTE OF WAR AND WINNINGS OF INDUSTRY.

WE have recently considered the capacities and burdens of the leading nations of Christendom; and noticed the great disproportion of the expenditures for war, compared with those for the purposes of civil government. In the case of Great Britain, especially, this disparity is the most extraordinary. The expenditures of that power, for wars past and prospective, in 1854, were more than 251,000,000 dollars; while all its other expenses amounted only to a little more than 30,000,000 dollars. It is difficult to convey to the common mind even an approximate idea of the values represented in these one hundred million amounts. It may assist the reader to their appreciation, if we measure them with familiar standards. To do this with the annual revenue of the richest man on earth, would be like measuring the equator with a two-foot rule. Let us take the largest joint-stock property in the world for our measure. This is the capital invested in railways in Great Britain, amounting, at the beginning of 1853, to £264,165,680, or 1,267,995,264 dollars. Every dollar of this almost unfathomable sum has been actually raised and paid in. Whoever has seen a modern map of the United Kingdom will have noticed that it is almost literally put in irons, or covered with such a net-work of railroads that the meshes of unintersected land look very small. Those who have travelled in that country must have been struck with the standing army of officials and men in fustian sustained by every line. Well, what are the gross earnings of all these railways in a good year? Why, in 1854 the whole receipts for passengers and freight amounted to £20,000,522, or 96,002,520 dollars. The reader will easily see, that this is the greatest vested interest on the face of the globe, ex-cluding landed estate. The annual income it produces far exceeds the revenue of any other investment in any single nation. Now put this and that together, and see what a lesson may be derived from the comparison. The expenditures of Great Britain in 1854, on mere preparations for war, were 117,984,201 dollars, and the gross receipts of all the railways of the kingdom that year, were 96,002,520 dollars; or nearly 22,000,000 dollars less than the amount appropriated to military and naval armaments!

Let us measure this annual offering to the altar of Mars by the standard of human labour and its earnings. The number of agricultural labourers, male and female, young and old, employed in Great Britain, in 1851, according to the census of that year, was 1,077,627.

Of this number 198,226 were under the age of twenty years; and probably one-third of these were under twelve. The average wages of able-bodied men is about ten English shillings per week. Taking with them the women and children in a general estimate, the average weekly wages of the whole number employed in farm-work would probably be seven shillings, or 1.68 dollars; making about £18. 4s., or eighty-seven dollars a year per head. Thus all the men, women, and children, who make Great Britain one great garden in beauty and wealth of production, earn £10,612,811, or 94,250,000 dollars in the course of twelve months, provided they all work every day in the year except the Sabbath. This is a large amount. But let us put this and that together. In round numbers, for producing food for man and beast, 96,250,000 dollars. There is a useful lesson at once apparent in the collocation of these figures. We would commend it to the honest toilers who plough, sow, and reap, and bear the out-door burden and brunt of feeding a nation. The deduction and inference are perfectly simple and easy to the mind of a child. For the husbandry of the plough, 94,259,000 dollars; for the husbandry of the sword, 118,000,000 dollars per annum !

Let us apply a measure to these vast expenditures for war in time of peace, which the commercial community will more fully appreciate. No nation in the world has ever done so much to open up new markets for its commerce as Great Britain. Its geographical situation has greatly favoured this policy; having, as it were, its factories and warehouses midway between the great continents of Asia, Africa, and Australia, and the whole of the Western Hemisphere. The whole globe is belted or dotted with its colonies; and these are all maritime, or accessible by water. To supply them all with manufactured goods and other productions, one would think should employ the industrial genius and activities of a great nation. But their trade is trifling compared with her commerce with independent States. In 1853 the imports of the United States amounted to 267,978,647 dollars; and 143,019,260 dollars, or more than half of this amount, came from Great Britain and its dependencies. She imports for manufactures more raw cotton, silk, and flax than all the other nations of Europe put together. The entire cellar of her island seems to be stocked with an inexhaustible supply of iron, coal, &c., and whole districts are covered with factories, dunning the heavens with smoke and dinning the ears of millions with the click and clatter of machinery. In the background of these manufacturing industries, or in the agricultural districts, is a boundless supply of cheap labour, from which they may be recruited at any time and to any extent. With such resources, there is no reason to wonder that Great Britain has surpassed all other nations in productive capacity. Her exports in 1854 amounted to 466,000,000 dollars; while those of the United States were 278,000,000 dollars, including specie. This comparison will show how far in advance of any other country she is in foreign commerce. Now, what is the net and positive profit of all these exports, after deducting every charge and liability? Is there any experienced merchant in New York or Boston who would put it at twenty-five per cent.? But let us allow that rate, which would make the total profit of 466,000,000 dollars amount to 116,500,000 dollars. Put this and that together. In 1854, there were 31,517 ships, with an aggregate burthen of 7,583,611 tons, that cleared from the ports of the United Kingdom, more or less freighted with its productions. The whole net profit of these was 116,500,000 dollars. The preparations for war the same year cost the nation 118,000,000 dollars! The merchant needs no suggestion in reference to the lesson these two facts convey. He will see at once the bearing and burden of the present armed-peace system upon the interests of commerce.

In the foregoing comparisons, we have had to do only with what are called peace establishments, or ordinary preparations for future hostilities. We have not touched upon the waste of actual war. Let us glance at one tide-mark which the deluge of this calamity has left as an instructive memento to the nations it has inundated. The Public Debts of all the States in Christendom, both in Europe and America, from which we have any official returns, amount to the grand total of 8,861,694,000 dollars. Undoubtedly, 8,000,000,000 dollars of this

almost immeasurable sum represent the war-bills left
to present and future generations to pay by those who
contracted them. What known value shall we apply to
this mountainous aggregate? What shall we put in the
opposite scale in order to ascertain its weight upon
the people of the civilized world? According to Otto
Hubner, the paid-up capital of the known banks of the
world amounted, in 1852, to 1,085,478,664 thalers, or
781,554,865 dollars. Thus, the war-debts of Christendom amount, at this moment, to ten times the capital
of all its banks! Here is a fact and a lesson for the
capitalist. He will see at once the reason why the
barometer of the public funds is so exceedingly sensitive;
sinking at a statesman's frown, or at an angry word
between two diplomatists. What is the meaning of all
these feverish perturbations in national securities may be
a puzzling query to common minds, unacquainted with
the true reason of the phenomenon; but to him it is all
clear as the day. Translating the true cause from the
delicate and mincing phraseology of " 'Change," it is
just this, and nothing more nor less. The monetary world
knows that " it is the last ounce that breaks the camel's
back;" that the people of Europe are now bending
towards the ground, and staggering under as heavy a
load as they can carry, and that a few more ounces will
break them down, and then, woe to all who have their
treasures in that crushing burden. It should be remembered that we have taken these war-debts as they existed

before this terrible and aimless conflict with Russia, just terminated by the Paris Conference. At the lowest figure admissible, this will add at least 1,000,000,000 dollars to the indebtedness of the various Powers that took part in it, directly or indirectly. Thus Christendom enters upon the first years of the last half of the nineteenth century with unpaid war-bills amounting to 9,000,000,000 dollars, besides other liabilities. What a legacy for future generations!

But the most aggravating circumstance connected with this appalling inheritance is the fact, that in some cases it will go down to them with the solemn and reiterated assurance of those who contracted it, or of their representatives, that it was all a mistake, and might have been avoided, had not the people been wrought up to a gust of passion and frenzy. Lord John Russell, Disraeli, and other eminent statesmen, representing all parties in the British Parliament, have deliberately declared their opinion to the world, from the high places they occupy, that the long wars with the French Republic and Empire were all waged upon a wrong principle, and might have been safely and honourably avoided. These wars cost the people of Great Britain about 5,000,000,000 dollars in money, besides a loss of human life money cannot measure. How tantalizing to be told, within fifty years of their termination, that all this sacrifice was for nothing; resulting in no real good to the nation, establishing no principle of justice! It required almost the life-time of a generation to get their eyes open to this stupendous delusion of all their first hopes, expectations, and objects in connexion with these long and bloody struggles.

Here, then, the nations of Christendom will enter upon 1857 with an aggregate of war-debts alone amounting to 9,000,000,000 dollars in round numbers. This does not, by any means, represent the waste of war during the last century, but that portion of its cost that is handed down unpaid. Doubtless the present generation will follow in the footsteps of its illustrious predecessor, and pass down this burden undiminished to unborn millions. But the interest must be paid annually. There is no way to wriggle out of that obligation. This interest, at five per cent., will amount to 450,000,000 dollars yearly. This sum, raised from the industry and earnings of the people, will serve to remind them impressively of their obligations to wars past. Then there is a considerable bill for wars prospective, or possible, which they have to meet annually. We cannot say within 50,000,000 dollars how much the actual preparations for war in Christendom cost in time of peace; for we have official returns from only twenty of the forty-three independent States which mostly comprise the family of civilized nations. These twenty include all the large Powers in Europe and America; and we find their annual expenditures for armies and navies amounted, in the aggregate, in 1854, to 466,000,000 dollars. The

expenses of the twenty-three small States, from which we
have no returns, would probably swell the sum to the
grand total of 500,000,000 dollars. It will be seen, that
these two great totals pretty nearly balance each other;
just as those probably did between which the ass, in
Scripture, crouched to the ground. Put together, and
reducing them to their minimum, they weigh 900,000,000
dollars. This is the annual tax imposed by war, past
and prospective, upon the people of the civilized world.
This is the amount which they must pay out of their
earnings every year to sate the cravings of that horse-
leech monster that cries, " Give ! give ! "

Nine hundred millions of dollars a year for wars past·
and possible ! What wonder there is a tremor in public
securities at the slightest danger that this mountainous
burden may become " the last ounce " too heavy for
the people's back ! It now exceeds by more than
100,000,000 dollars the paid-up capital of the banks
in the world. It is equal to the aggregate exports of
England, France, and the United States, and to full fifty
per cent. of the exports of all the nations of the world.
It is twice the rental of all the real estate of Great
Britain; it exceeds the net profit of all the manufacturers
of Christendom. It is equal to the annual wages of
4,500,000 agricultural labourers at 200 dollars per head.
It would pay for the construction of 45,000 miles of
railway at 20,000 dollars per mile. It would support
1,200,000 ministers of the gospel, allowing each 750

dollars per annum; giving a religious teacher and pastor to every 750 persons of the whole population of the globe.

Such is the condition of the people of Christendom in 1856, resulting from the Waste of War.

—o—o—

THE PENNY POST OF ENGLAND.

THE citizen of a foreign country, sojourning in England, cannot fail to be struck with its extraordinary capacity of society. Let him travel the world over, and he will not find twenty millions of individuals possessing such faculties and facilities of social intercourse as are enjoyed by the inhabitants of Great Britain. Time and space, which divide and half estrange the communities of other countries, are hardly known here, in the sense of separation. All the homes of England are not only in conversational distance of each other, but of London—that great city-centre, which, by its commercial attractions inhales, as it were, into its bosom all the intelligence that floats in isolated facts over the surface of the world. And the little time lost in overcoming the spaces between these homes, so far as the most important part of their intercourse is concerned, is lost in the night, and, with it, the sense of its duration. The machinery by which this is achieved is truly marvellous in all its operations; especially to an American, or to the citizen of a country covering a vast extent of territory. The working of this machinery, in one direction, is somewhat after this fashion:

At about nine o'clock in the evening, several iron horses may be seen, harnessed for their race, at each of the five railway stations in London. There they stand, foaming, neighing, and champing their bridle-bits, with their heads turned in different directions, impatient for the signal to be gone. But who can fathom the mystery of the mail bags which they are to bear, as upon the wings of the wind, and to distil on their way to tens of thousands of home-circles scattered over the kingdom? Never could dewdrops or raindrops quote a more vicissitous experience than the letters or other messages of business or friendship, collected in these same mail bags. Never were clouds filled with waterdrops drawn from such distant and diversified sources. For, among the myriads of these epistolatory messages drawn from the metropolis and the provinces, may be found thousands from China, the Indies, the Pacific and Atlantic Islands, the Americas, and all the continents of the Old World.

The five railway stations are the five gates of the metropolis, from which this mass of sealed intelligence is to be distilled consentaneously with the dew of heaven, over the whole of England, before the rising of the sun. The fiery chargers are neighing upon their iron track. The penny postmen have mounted; the signal is given.

Each huge courser bates the explosions of his fiery breath, as if to listen to his driver's voice, and the next moment treads out slowly into the night. Snorting a fierce defiance at time and space, he dashes into the deepening thunder of the race. Now the tunneled hills tremble and groan sepulchrally, as he plows his track of fire through their old foundations, and fills the arched breach with smoke. Now the still and rural villages, with churches old and quaint, and cottages thatched with straw, revolve with their low glimmering lights, and all the tall trees go around with them in stately procession, as the iron horse plunges onward, with his fiery eye-balls glaring upon the track before him.

At midnight, and thence until morning, there is silence in the habitations of human life, and slumber is on the eyelids of the million. Love and its deep-seated and various affections, which dream but seldom slumber, are dreaming now perhaps of distant ones in the great metropolis, or on the other side of the kingdom, or, perchance, in India, New Zealand, or in the scattered colonies of the distant seas. In that straw-roofed cottage, slumbering like a weary labourer behind the hedge, are human thoughts of great affection that are stealing out of the hearts of toil-worn sleepers, and feeling their way across the Atlantic to the new homes of children they will see no more on earth. And in the ivy-curtained chambers of yonder house, with its windows peeping at the moon through the still trees, boyhood is dreaming of

boyhood in the playgrounds of distant schools, and girlhood is weaving flower-bracelets again with girlhood, or
dancing along the silver brooks in meadows and pastures
far beyond the bluest hills. In the silence and unre-
membered emotions of the mind slumber the age and
infancy and all the conditions of a nation. But those
chariots of fire are running like lightning through all
these dark and quiet hours, exchanging with each other
a part of their respective charges, and dispensing to
thousands of sleeping towns, villages, and hamlets, a
portion which shall gladden their family circles in the
morning. And the morning comes, and with it comes
to thousands and hundreds of thousands the wonderful
reality wrought from the mystery of all this fiery loco-
motion of the night. To thousands of home-circles, in
town, village, hamlet, and by hedge-side, the dispensation
of the Penny Post comes almost as gratuitously and as
silently as that of the morning dew upon the flowers that
blush and breathe in their windows. The American so-
journer, who may be the guest of one of these English
homes, if he has a heart open to the susceptibilities of
our social nature, must comprehend the joy which the
Penny Post diffuses around the table at breakfast. For,
associating its beneficence with enjoyments most necessary to nature, it serves up its messages of love and
friendship as condiments to the morning meal. The
administration of the tea-urn, under the presidency of
the lady of the house, commences at the same time as

that of the Penny Post at the other end of the table. For the servant girl has brought in, on the same tray with the dry toast, a packet of letters and papers, which she deals out, simultaneously with the brown slices of bread, to the different members of the circle. The relish of this double repast is the refinement of that social enjoyment which England has procured for her millions, in giving them the blessings of cheap postage. " Sunbeam of summer, what is like thee ? " sung a sweet spirit, whose poetry was the breath of flowers. Had she lived to witness the light of gladness which Rowland Hill's great boon diffuses every morning through thousands of English homes, she might have answered : " One thing is like thee — it is the PENNY POST, carrying into yearning hearts rays of affection from hearts beating beyond the mountains and the seas; touching the faces of the aged, of the matron, maiden, and child, with a light which the sunbeam of summer cannot give."

Look at that family at this moment of social enjoyment. " You will please excuse us, sir, for glancing at our letters," observes the host. " That I will, my dear sir, and wish you all much joy of it." The tea will bear to stand a moment longer; and now you may steal a glance kindly at the faces of the circle surrounding the table, as they open and read the messages addressed to them. The letters of mine host are evidently more of a business cast than others; some bringing across his countenance an involuntary expression of thoughtfulness, others stirring up the momentary semblance of a smile. But there is the communion of other thoughts going on at the other end of the table. " Sunbeam of summer, what is like thee ? " if it is not the light that glistens in that mother's eye, as she drinks in the words of affection contained in that letter from a young married daughter, in the metropolis, three hundred miles distant, who penned them last evening just before tea. And by the side of her mother sits the younger sister of the distant one; and a " sunbeam of summer " is deepening the rose in her cheeks, as she reads with parted lips the message which the Penny Post has brought to her from a boarding-school companion, who has enclosed a little spring flower in her letter, still breathing its sweetness on the loving thoughts she has put into words. And Fred, frolicsome, laughter-loving Fred, although scarcely seven, has a letter, which he reads with eyes growing bigger every moment—a letter from his cousin Willy, and no secret would he make of it, were the Duke of Wellington by his father's side. " Willy has got another rabbit, with the funniest ears that a rabbit ever had ; and Towzer broke his chain and chased the ducks into the pond; and papa has bought a new saddle for the pony, with stirrups that look like silver; and there will be beautiful skating if the water will be good enough to freeze; and he has put three pheasant's eggs under the speckled hen; and "—" Why, Freddy ! " whispers his sister, bending toward him, and glancingly apologetically toward you. "Frederic, my dear," softly adds his mother, looking too lovingly at the boy to mean reproof—"You will please excuse our Frederic, sir; he and his cousin Willy are schoolmates, and always together, except in vacation." And the servant girl has not been forgotten in this dispensation of the Penny Post; there are those at a distance, perhaps in New Zealand or Newfoundland, who remember her with fraternal or sisterly affection; and she carries a letter in her bosom, which she reads in the kitchen whilst watching the toast, and which she will read again before sunset.

Such is the daily experience of an English family. Such is the social enjoyment which seasons the morning meal of thousands and tens of thousands, as one of the blessings of the Penny Post. To procure for them this luxury, these thundering steeds of iron have run to and fro all the night long. What an issue of all this loco-motion! One would be inclined to believe that there was a post-office in every Englishman's kitchen, of which the servant maid was the mistress; for almost every morning she is sure to serve up, on her toast-tray, letters from different parts of the kingdom. For scarcely a portion of the machinery of this beautiful administration is visible to the family it gladdens. Perhaps they heard, or dreamed they heard, at midnight, the distant sound of the iron horse as he shook the earth with his tread. Perhaps they heard the postman's knock at the door; but even him they seldom see. We know of no institution of human legislation so like GOD's gifts to man, as the English Penny Post. Like the quality of mercy in His grace and salvation, it is not strained, nor limited to any class or condition of the community. The quiet joy which it diffuses every morning through thousands of family circles, is like a dew of gladness, falling alike upon the rich and poor, the palace and the cottage. If there be a blessing which a patriot, philanthropist, or Christian could wish for his country, after the light of GOD's countenance and gospel, and the dispensations of the seasons, it might well be the PENNY POST.

—◦—◦—

EIGHTEEN HUNDRED AND FIFTY-THREE.

A NEW Year! and a happy one may it be to humanity, unfolding from the rustling curtain of its invisible experience, realities exceeding in beneficence any that shone upon the world during the year that has gone away into the slumber and silence of the past. A New Year! Eighteen hundred and fifty-three! How sounds the number of that graduating point of time? It has a mounting intonation, as if the march of mankind lay over some mighty St. Bernard of observation, whose summit commands the vista of unseen years and the images of distant events reflecting in the still, blue future. Eighteen hundred and fifty-three! It has a climbing sound, and falls upon the ear like an *Excelsior!* Then a happy new year to all who look, long, and labour for the good time coming. "*E pure si muove*"—"Still it moves"—burst from the lips of Galileo, while repeating on his knees before the cardinals of Rome the recantation of the heretical doctrine of the earth's motion. And "Still it moves" may be seen and said of the moral world, even in its cloudiest aspects. It moves forward toward those peaceful and happy conditions predicted and promised in divine revelation. They are all included within the boundary of humanity. They shall be reached and realized on this very earth. There shall come a time—and a busy time it will be, we opine, and full of energy—when "nation shall not lift up sword against nation, neither shall they learn war any more." And for all that, the ocean will swarm with gigantic steamships, railways girdle the globe, and the electric telegraph nerve it with netted lines of carrier lightning. None of the great activities of mighty nations will droop for lack of martial stimulus. The dockyards of commerce and the arsenals of beneficent industry will lose none of their hum, though no ship be built for war, nor iron shaped for human slaughter. The time shall come—and a busy time it shall be—when the knowledge of GOD shall cover the earth as the waters cover the sea; when all its antagonistic nationalities, tribes, and tongues shall be fused into one peaceful and perpetual brotherhood; when the last fetter of slavery shall be broken, and the oppressed go free.

And for all this, the indestructible attachments and affinities planted in human nature will live and act on — acting in the sublime harmony of the world as varying notes in music. The love of home, of country, and all the concentric series of human affections will live on and act—acting like tenor strings to those of deeper bass in the universal anthem of " Glory to GOD in the highest, on earth peace, and good-will among men ! " That time shall come, not as a thief in the night, not as a friend in the night. It shall come like the low, soft dawn in spring. It shall be seen and blessed by the watchers of that hallowed morning, from the first faint tint to the bursting glory of its brightness. That time shall come, for the mouth of the LORD has spoken it ; and that settles the matter. It will come with its great anthem of " Glory to GOD in the highest ; " and those will sing it with the greatest joy and humility whom He has permitted to co-work with Him in hastening its advent.

THE SENTIMENT OF NATIONALITY.

IT is with a lively sense of the delicacy of the subject that we approach the question of " Nationalities." The hereditary sentiments of mankind, for five thousand years, have surrounded these political entities with a halo of sacred associations. The scattered and confounded Babel-builders, who essayed, against the Divine Will, to site and citadel a nationality that should fill the whole earth, at their dispersion fell to the erection of humbler towers, each crowned with lofty aspirations; each containing its ever-burning altar, on which patriotism poured the incense of its love, hope, and faith. " Let us make *us* a name " was the watchword and workword of the great primeval community which assembled on the plain of Shinar. " Let us make *us* a name " has been the motto and the motive-aspiration of every tribe or clan, of every age, race, and language, whether it burrowed itself by night in the sands of Sahara, or in the snows of Siberia; whether it kindled its camp-fire under the shadow of the Rocky Mountains, or of the Himalaya, or of Hecla. " Make *us* a name." Herein is the secret of this everlasting and universal ambition of the human heart. Not make *me*, but *us* a name. We would touch this germ-sentiment tenderly; not *me*, but *us*. Translate it: " *Me* is a short-lived personality; *I* must soon die, and the place *I* occupy shall know me no more. Come, then, fellow-mortal individualities, let us unite and construct a nationality that shall live for centuries. Let us build an immortal WE, which shall walk abroad on the earth in glory when our individual ashes shall have mingled with the dust. What is *thy* name or *my* name? What is it but a passing shadow, a footprint in the morning dew—seen for a moment, then gone for ever! Come, let us make us a collective name, which our posterity, to the latest generation, shall inherit and cherish as the charter and guarantee of everlasting remembrance among men."

To no sentiment of the human heart has the race yielded more general and enthusiastic homage than to this. Whatever diverse habits and dispositions distinguished their wandering or divided communities, this collective name-building retained every characteristic of its original attraction. The earth has been covered with *We's*, varying in compass of association from the wandering clan to the multitudinous nationality. For centuries, these small communities clung to their independent existence, with all the glowing fervour and strength of patriotism. To merge one with another to form a larger We, was to extinguish a collective name and being, around which had clustered the hopes and affections of many a generation.

These natural and interesting sentiments made the work of amalgamation a slow and difficult process, even in the most thickly-populated and enlightened countries. Long after a nominal union had taken place, and the collective circle had been doubled in circumference, the old clan or feudal feeling would show itself strong and ardent, and cling with tenacity to a family or community-name which it seemed suicide to extinguish. Look at those countries that have lived longest under the meridian sun of civilization. Glance at the history of France and Great Britain. How many centuries it

required to reduce the petty nationalities of England to
seven distinct, independent kingdoms, without counting
those in Wales and Scotland! Look at France at the
same time. Nearly every large town was the capital
of a sovereign principality or barony that could wage
war against its neighbours. How desperately every one
of these miniature nations stood out against the idea of
merging its individuality in a larger combination! How
loudly patriotism rebelled and remonstrated against the
act! Had the art of printing been then in operation,
what bursts of fervid eloquence against these ruinous
annexations would have been handed down to us!
Even at the present moment, some of the Scottish clans
in the Highlands stand out in sentiment against the
extinction of their feudal or tribe-name. They still cling
to the semblance of distinct communities, and perhaps
retain a little of the old feeling which existed five
hundred years ago towards each other. Notwithstanding
the oneness of language, religion, interests, and all the
network of railways and electric telegraphs, which would
seem to unite and identify all the populations of Great
Britain, Scotland still retains some of the features and
functions and more of the sentiment of an independent
nationality. With its full share in legislating for the
empire, it has and makes, to a great degree, its own
distinctive laws. Even in the matter of customs or
excise regulations, it possesses certain peculiar prerogatives which distinguish it from England, and give it an

aspect of independent sovereignty. Up to within a
very recent period, if it does not now exist, a regulation
was in force for examining the luggage of railway passengers from Scotland at Carlisle, the first station on the
English side of the line, with the view of preventing
the smuggling of Scottish spirits into England. This
search was almost as rigid as that which is imposed upon
travellers crossing the boundary between Belgium and
France; and it suggested the same idea of two different
countries and governments. And, in fact, it is doubtful
whether any people in Christendom ever had the feeling
of nationality developed and stimulated to such intense
enthusiasm as the Scotch. Their border warfares with
the English were waged with as fierce a spirit as that
which marked the crusades of the same period, and, to
all outward seeming, the Christians and Saracens were
as likely to unite and constitute one people and government, as were these hereditary and mutual enemies,
occupying an island hardly surpassing in extent the territory of New York and Pennsylvania. For centuries,
they preferred to ally themselves to France, rather than
to the " Southrons," towards whom they seemed to
entertain the most implacable hostility. Even to hunt
bears or hares beyond the boundary line was as much a
casus belli between the borderers as it would have been
between two hostile tribes of North-American Indians.

Still the history of England and Scotland and that of
other countries have shown that this sentiment of nation-

ality, however ardent and strong, may be conciliated and embodied even as an element of union, in expanding the great circles of human society. The feeling is not exhausted by this expansion, but embraced within the circumference of another equally dear to the heart of patriotism. The infant this day born to the arms of the Highland cotter, when he comes to manhood, will not love Scotland less, as the land of his nativity, because he is also a born subject of the British Empire, and feels himself politically related to all the millions that live under its sceptre, in different portions of the globe. While his filial affections and associations cling fondly and strongly to the inner circle of his birth-land, the sentiment of nationality will reach outward, beyond seas and oceans, to the most remote colony or dependency of that empire; and, with a species of personal as well as patriotic pride, he will feel himself one of the vast and multitudinous We upon which the sun never sets. Look in almost every direction, and you will find this sentiment susceptible of the same expansion. In some countries, this has been carried almost to an extreme, apparently. For instance, the old independent, antagonistic, or rival sovereignties and principalities of France have become so completely merged and consolidated in one compact nationality, that the feeling which once attached each so intensely to its own political name and entity, is now hardly perceptible, even if it has a latent existence. How little one travelling through that country hears of the distinct traditions and heroics of Normandy, Navarre, or Burgundy! The patriotic sentiment seems to have overflown these inner, private circles of its attachment, and to have embraced the "Grand Empire," the "Great Republic," "La Belle France," in its vast oneness and integrity.

Look at Germany, with all its independent sovereignties, now confederated coherently under one imperial sceptre, now resolved into separate, rival, and hostile states. They have all passed through a period of bitter antagonisms, and warred with each other after the English and Scotch fashion. They are not united now. Still, though every German heart clings to some one of those states with special attachment, it swells with larger patriotism towards the great Fatherland; and Germany, as a unity, as one grand federal nationality, is the beau ideal of his aspiration.

Turn to the United States. Here we have the same sentiment of nationality in two concentric circles of life and manifestation. The first compasses a particular State. Its very name is associated with cherished memories and affections. This is "my native State." What American heart is insensible to the thoughts and feelings these few words suggest! But why should it cherish such sentiments towards such a large circle as a State, or the fiftieth part of one vast continent? "This house is my birthplace; this is my native town;" are terms which describe the most intimate relations to a special locality. "All these hills and valleys, trees and brooks I looked upon and loved from childhood to manhood. All the inhabitants of this village and neighbourhood I have known from their youth or middle age. These circumstances make these particular three square miles dear to me. This is my native town." Very good. That is clear and natural. But why do you then say, "This is my native State," which contains a hundred towns, half of which you have never seen, and never will see in all probability? What birth-relation do you sustain to this arbitrary territory, and to all its towns and their inhabitants? "A political birth-relation. I am a birth-right member of the great community inheriting, inhabiting, and governing this State. They and I make a distinct and peculiar We; and we 'make us a name,' laws, institutions, and do other things for our own special good and well-being. I am a Vermonter, or a Virginian. That is the collective name of a hundred thousand families, and we hope and believe it will live for a thousand years, if the earth abides so long."

Here is the inner circle of patriotism; its private homestead as it were. What man or woman, from California to Canada, cannot attest to the existence and strength of this feeling! We do not believe that there is a country in the world where this primary manifestation of the national sentiment is so striking and distinct as in America. In order to domesticate State attachments, and make each more personal or special, terms

of endearment are introduced, or names descriptive of
peculiar qualities.   Thus we have the affectionate di-
minutive of " Little Rhody," for Rhode Island; the
" Old Bay State," the " Old Granite State," the " Key-
stone State," the " Empire State," &c.   To hear these
appellations repeated everywhere, inscribed on banners
and mounted upon large capitals in the newspapers, a
foreigner might be inclined to think that the foremost
ambition of an American citizen was to uplift the individuality of his own State to the highest elevation and
prominence possible; that the most of his patriotism
beat only within this inner circle; and that the sentiment
of larger nationality was correspondingly weak and taci-
turn.   But let him travel a little further and see a little
more clearly, and he will soon recognize an immense
manifestation of this sentiment.   Not a man, woman, or
child will he meet between the two oceans, who is not
deeply impressed with the grandeur and glory of the
Nation.   As State after State is added to the Union,
and star after star to its banner, the American feeling
becomes more and more intense, instead of being diluted.
The Vermonter or Virginian may often and fondly expa-
tiate upon the " Green Mountain State," or the " Old
Dominion," as the home of his heart, but touch it with
the mention of the great Union, of its history, hopes,
and expansion, and, with an emotion of patriotism, as
proud as the old Roman's, he will say, " I am an
American Citizen."   No living man of any name or

nation could speak of a political birthright with more honest pride than swells his bosom at the thought of his relationship to all the past, present, and future of the American Republic. With all the individual State attachments that exist, this feeling of nationality is as complete and unanimous as if the Federal Union were consolidated and centralized to the oneness of France itself; as if American patriotism had but one circle and centre within and around which to revolve.

Thus we see that the sentiment of nationality, so strong and jealous in the heart of humanity, needs neither to be extinguished nor offended permanently by enlarging the sphere of its action. We say, permanently; for doubtless that sentiment was wounded keenly for the moment, when all the Saxon kingdoms in England were united under one sceptre. Doubtless there were vigorous and eloquent denunciations of this act at the time; and the terms, "treachery, suicide, corruption, selling your country, becoming vassals, paying tribute," &c., were loud-spoken and abundant. A louder remonstrance arose, and more vehement antagonism, at the next stage of annexation and expansion, or when successively Wales, Scotland, and Ireland were united with England, to compose with her one imperial realm. How all the wild pathos of Welsh bards deplored this union, and stirred up their countrymen against it! Then the Scotch took up the same strain; and all their mountain bagpipes were ready to burst with heroic patriotism

s

against parting with one iota of their local sovereignty. As for the Irish, they are piping still against the act of union. It is probable that most of these antagonisms opposed the union of those once rival kingdoms and principalities which now compose the French Empire. We admit, therefore, that the absorption of small independent nationalities into larger combinations cannot be effected without exciting unhappy sensibilities at the time being. But these sensibilities are generally caused, not by the act of union, but by the condition of separation that preceded it; therefore they cannot endure long. For example, the kilted Highlander might have exclaimed, "What! give up my native land, and unite with England, and become only a portion, a segment of Great Britain!" The sentiment of nationality is touched to an indignant emotion in his breast. But he forgets an important circumstance: he speaks as if all his posterity would stand in his position at that moment, and sustain his relationship. He forgets that the first child born to him after the act of union will not only be a native of Scotland, but of Great Britain; that, further on, the grandchild of that child, instead of being the henchman of some lairdly clan-leader or clan-owner in the Highlands, may stand in the imperial parliament of a great empire, and vote the extinction of feudalism throughout its borders.

However we may respect the sensibilities which at first revolt at the idea of merging or uniting one nation-

ality with another, they should not be admitted as
decisive arguments against such a step. How will the
proposed union affect the well-being of the generations
born after the act? is the most important question to be
considered, not how it will affect the passing predilections
of those about leaving the stage. It is an act for posterity—a provision for a distant future. As such, will it
work well for all parties and interests? When the united
communities shall really and truly become one in sympathy; when the territories they now occupy shall become
one and the same native land to all who are born in
either; when they shall make their past history a
common stock of remembrance, and their hopes for
the future a common source of faith and courage; when
they shall sit down together, as it were, under the vine
and fig tree of one political condition— the work of
their united mind and legislation—will they be wiser,
happier, and better for the connexion? That is the
question which should weigh most upon the citizen of
the world, in forming his opinion of such a transaction.
If all those desirable ends are likely to be realized by
the union of hitherto independent states or principalities,
he should not withhold his approval of the act because
it may excite a temporary ebullition of that hereditary
sentiment which revolts at parting with a feature of
nationality. He may rest assured that no injustice will
be done to this feeling; that it will neither be extinguished nor weakened, but, on the other hand,

enlightened and expanded to embrace a wider sphere of influence; to live and act in nobler manifestations.

Having thus briefly considered the Sentiment of Nationality, and shown, we would hope, to some of our readers, that no wrong needs be done to this interesting feeling, in uniting different states and peoples in one political system, we reserve for another article the discussion of other bearings of this important question.

---❖—❖---

THE RIGHT AND DIGNITY OF NATIONALITY.

WE have considered the sentiment of nationality, and traced its origin and its working upon the human mind. We are confident that most of our readers who participated with us in this investigation, must be convinced that independent States may unite with each other and form one undivided people, without wrong or detriment to this sentiment, although it is one of the strongest feelings that ever throbbed in the heart of humanity. We have seen that some of the most antagonistic populations have been thus amalgamated and identified under one government; as, for example, those of Scotland, England, and Wales. In these and other cases, the sentiment of nationality, so far from being weakened or wronged in the end, acquired new strength, compass, and elevation. If such unions or annexations could be consummated in an age when Christendom was but slowly emerging from the shades of barbarism, and was still under the dominion of malignant jealousies, hereditary hatreds, and religious bigotries, is there not every reason to believe that far larger combinations may be effected, to the mutual happiness and prosperity of the countries thus united, in these more enlightened times? That is the question which we would now submit to the candid consideration of our readers.

We would approach this important question with all proper deference to those wide-spread popular opinions which are directly opposed to the views we shall present. The aspect of the subject which we would now commend to our readers may be limited to the right and dignity of nationality. It is a delicate and difficult undertaking, to treat with due reverence and sincere impartiality a subject so fraught and surrounded with the liveliest sensibilities of human nature itself. And were not the motive, and spirit, and object of such an inquiry manifestly legal and true to the well-being of mankind, it would be reprehensible, even as a philosophical investigation. But we believe an inquiry instituted with such a motive and in such a spirit cannot be premature or irrelevant to this remarkable juncture of human affairs. And, we trust, the standpoint from which an impartial citizen of the world would consider this delicate question could not be offensive to the tenderest sensibility of patriotism. This standpoint must always be a little more remote from the subject to be examined than that from which it is viewed by the immediate parties to the question. Interests and principles of wider range must be admitted into the sphere of vision.

Now, to many ardent patriots or partisans of some local polity, this may seem an unfeeling and ungenerous mode and motive of observation. Their own present and past are the two great links of their being and history; and the future they would have as like them in the chain as one link can be like another. They are the only actors within the sphere of to-day; and they would forge their own future and the future of their posterity. They would have the casting vote, wherewith to decide the political destiny of distant generations, to elect for those generations the nationality to which they shall belong, to prescribe the boundaries of their patriotism, to stereotype their own notions of race and country, to perpetuate for ever the prejudices and predilections of the present. Now, in estimating aright the real value of independent nationalities and the necessity of their separate existence, most of these ambitious pretensions must be set aside as worthless. The past and present are not time; nor does one generation constitute a nation. The preferences and patriotic associations of a people should not decide this estimate in the mind of one looking to the greatest good of the human family. A well-constructed nation ought to live to the last year of time, throughout all future generations on earth. If it be founded on the right principles and composed of the right elements, there is no reason why it should not be as lasting as the future life of humanity. We believe that every man in Christendom has a right to such a nationality, whatever be its name. He may not recognize that right: he may reject, and scorn, and hate it. He may prefer a name to a nation, and cling, with desperate tenacity, to the horns of that local altar on which he and his fathers have burnt the incense of their patriotism. He may throw his arms around the banner of a decadent people, and hug it to his breast, and say that no other shall ever wave over him or his remotest posterity; and all this because it bears the Polish, Hungarian, Italian, or Irish insignia. All this is interesting and admirable in him as a sentiment; but it should not affect the true value of his political right and dignity in the opinion of a disinterested mind, much less the political status and condition of his posterity. Their national destiny and associations ought not to be decided by his short-lived predilections and notions. Once the tartaned Highlander enfolded the banner of Scotland within his brawny arms with all the devotion with which the most chivalrous Pole or Hungarian could cling to his country's flag. But the grandson of that Highlander was born a Briton as well as a Scot; and Britain's banner he clasped to his heart, and made all its grand associations as much his own as did his grandsire those which clustered around the flag of Scotia. The descendant honours with his best homage that standard which his ancestor hated as an alien banner. Though born in his ancestral cottage, he is a native of that land, too, which his grandsire called the enemy's country.

Thus, in estimating the necessity and value of the union of England and Scotland, the current predilections and prejudices of the inhabitants of the two countries at the time of the transaction, must weigh but little upon the judgment of the impartial observer of to-day. And so it should be in considering the necessity and advantage of enlarging the nationalities of Europe by uniting those conterminous states which may be combined to the ultimate and inestimable benefit of their respective populations. What they themselves may feel, say, or think, in regard to such a union, should not at all affect our appreciation of its value to all the generations of their posterity. " Rome was not built in a day;" nor is a permanent nationality to be perfected in a century. It requires several generations to come and go, before populations thus united under one government become one in blood, soul, and sympathy. There are hundreds of good, sincere persons in the Welsh mountains who cannot yet speak the English language, and who still think that the union of their country with England was a suicidal transaction. There are thousands, perhaps millions, still in Ireland, who would rather regain their national independence than be part and parcel of the grand and powerful empire of Great Britain. But the candid and benevolent mind, looking upon the past, present, and future of these annexed populations, from beyond the circumference of their temporary predilections, will see that the union which they deplore will work immeasurably to the peace, prosperity, and true dignity of all the generations of their posterity.

We have said, that the discussion of this delicate question is not premature, nor irrelevant to this remarkable juncture of human affairs. We are confident that all who have watched, with intelligent eyes, the political phases and transactions of European Christendom during the past year, must admit this fact. They must be prepared to concede, at least, the desirability, if not the practicability, of permitting the natural law of combination to have its course—to attract, annex, and amalgamate, until at least half the present nominally independent states of Europe shall be absorbed into nationalities as nearly equal to each other in power, and dignity, and true sovereignty as possible. Now, this may startle or offend many a partisan of state rights; as if the realization of this proposition would swallow up and confound the patriotic aspirations of many a noble and heroic people, and merge the precious associations and souvenirs of their past in the river of an alien history. But on the very ground of state rights would we base the

argument for the amalgamation of European nationalities. The first right of an independent state is
sovereignty, intact, sacred, inviolate, and inviolable—
a sovereignty complete over its own volition and action
in regulating its own affairs; in every act of legislation
necessary to the well-being of its subjects; in adopting
its internal policy and its relations with other powers—a
sovereignty that shall be respected by other states, as an
equal ·in all the prerogatives of national independence.
This sovereignty is the immediate jewel of a nation's
soul; and if this be filched from it, or tarnished by
foreign influence, it is lifeless and worthless. This is
the great vital right of a state. Who questions or
doubts this? No one, we are confident. Then we
maintain that it is the unalienable right of every individual man in Christendom to belong to a nationality
possessing this sovereignty, and able to maintain it in all
its dignity. He may not recognize nor value this right
He may exchange it for a fiction, for a shadow, for a
song. But in regarding him as a political entity, we
must admit the existence of this right at its full
worth.

Now look at the condition of the people of Europe at
this moment. There are at least one hundred millions,
embracing many of its best educated populations, who
are living in a kind of political nihilation, because they
belong to nationalities whose sovereignty is virtually a
fiction. The present ordeal is demonstrating this painful

fact most conclusively. Even those States which have made a great show of independence, and of vast military armaments to support it, have been weighed and found wanting of the true dignity of national sovereignty. For instance, look at the attitude, and listen to the language adopted by England and France towards Prussia, and even Austria, in relation to this Eastern Question! What would an Englishman, a Frenchman, or a Russian say, if such deportment were assumed towards his country? What would either say to diplomatic games of chess played by rival foreign ambassadors in London, Paris, or St. Petersburgh for ascendant influence over the policy of his nation? Would not a subject of either of these three great States redden with indignation at even the suspicion of its sovereignty being tarnished with the breath of such foreign intermeddling? Look at Spain, Portugal, Belgium, Holland, Switzerland, Sardinia, Turkey, Denmark, and Sweden! What are they, one by one, in the scale of political being? What is the weight of their opinion or influence in any great question of European interest—in this Eastern Question, for example? What does a subject of either of those kingdoms stand for? what does he represent? what sentiment of national dignity swells his bosom as he journeys across the continent of Europe, and mingles with other populations? He may be as virtuous, intelligent, and patriotic as any subject of Great Britain or France. As a moral individual, he may be their equal, their superior.

But weighed in the scale of nationality, he is a mere feather to either of them; and, with all his glowing love of country and personal merit, he must feel this disparity of political valuation.

In the still and sunny years of peace, while the giants are asleep, these Tom Thumb nationalities may disport themselves in all the dreams of independent sovereignty, and be encouraged in the delusion. But let some great question arouse those dormant giants, and woe to the Lilliputian States that dare oppose their prerogatives to the colossal tread of the Anakim Powers. As these stalk onward to the goal of their interests or ambition, let no dog bark within the pale of the little nations; let no press therein animadvert or remonstrate; no cabinet evince antagonistic affinities; no people presume to side in sympathy with the party adverse to the "Great Powers."

"Oppressed Nationalities!" Their very existence is the tyrant that oppresses them; that reduces their subjects to a political nihilation. "Divide and conquer" was the march-word and policy of old Imperial Rome; "*in hoc signo vinces*," said the inspiration of her lawless ambition, and said it truly. She vanquished the known world of her day under the banner of this policy. The populations of more than half of Christendom have turned this policy against their own political being, by dividing themselves into impotent nationalities, which can never attain to the dignity of independent sovereignties. There is no disguising nor disputing the fact; for the events of the last twelve months have made it as clear as the sun: neither Prussia nor Austria is a self-standing, inviolable sovereignty; and neither can impart to its subjects that status and sentiment of national dignity to which, we maintain, every virtuous man in Christendom is entitled. There are only three capitals in Europe that are not the perpetual battle-grounds of foreign and rival diplomacy, caballing, planning, and plotting for predominant influence over the councils of the country. These great and distinguished metropoles are London, Paris, and St. Petersburgh. Let no one deem it a hard saying; for it is said in sorrow, and in sympathy with the people it affects: Great Britain, France, and Russia are the only nationalities in Europe that have attained to the dignity of full independent sovereignty, such as is maintained by the United States. Nor is that all. Those three are the only Powers in Europe that ever can attain to complete state sovereignty, until a large amalgamation of small nationalities shall be effected.

It was thought at the time a harsh, unfeeling remark of General Jackson, that " all who traded on borrowed capital ought to fail." Whoever may be disposed to doubt the truth and application of that observation, must admit that every State that "trades on borrowed capital," or leans upon foreign protection, and yields the helm of its sovereignty to the bias of foreign influence,

ought to fail, must fail, does fail of every attribute of
true national being and dignity. It cheats its subjects
with a delusion; it reduces them to a political valuation
which is contemned by populations perhaps inferior
to themselves in personal virtue and intelligence. And
we maintain this condition is not the one to which they
are entitled; but it is a condition from which they cannot escape, until they have conquered it by bursting the
bonds of contracted, oppressing nationality. That term
may offend some patriotic sensibilities; but we sincerely
believe that no other could describe so well and truth-
fully the cause of that condition of political nonentity
in which nearly one hundred millions of the inhabitants of Europe exist at this moment. In defence of
their inalienable right and dignity, we maintain that,
instead of lifting up and setting upon their legs any
new or half-decomposed nationalities, one-half of those
now existing in Europe should be extinguished by
absorption into larger combinations. Do any of our
readers doubt the necessity of this arrangement? Then
look at Spain, Sardinia, Greece, Turkey, and even Prussia
and Austria. Take the most hopeful aspect of the
future, and tell us in what distant year you think it may
be possible for the cabinets of Madrid, Rome, Athens,
Constantinople, Vienna, and Berlin to shake off the
subtle incubus of the " Great Powers " of England,
France, and Russia. Tell us when we may hope to see
those capitals no longer the game-grounds of foreign

diplomacy. Tell us when one hundred millions, occupying the very heart of Europe, shall, under the rule of their present nationalities, attain to that status and sentiment of political rank which those Three Powers give to their subjects. Perhaps we may attach more value than most of our readers to this inalienable right of every man to State sovereignty. But we would ask, is there an American heart beating between the Atlantic and Pacific that would not rather see our great Republic annexed to Russia to-morrow, than to live the political life that Turkey has lived, under foreign influence, for the last quarter of a century? Is there a man born within the compass of our Union who would not spurn with indignation a nationality helmed at Washington by foreign diplomacy? It is in our heart to say it, and say it we will: Better be conquered than "protected." Better be part of a great Whole, than the whole of a little Nothing.

—o—c—

THE PHYSIOLOGY AND UNION OF NATIONALITIES.

WE have considered the sentiment and dignity of nationality, and seen that both may be elevated and enlarged by the union of conterminous states under one government. We will now proceed to examine those obstacles and objections to this amalgamation, which, in many minds, seem to be almost insuperable.

We hope none of our readers, on calm, dispassionate reflection, have deemed presumptuous, fanciful, or erroneous the views we have advanced on the right and dignity of nationality. At first, it may have sounded like a rash assertion, to say, as we have said, that there are only *three* Powers in Europe possessing and exercising all the prerogatives of complete independent sovereignty. But we are persuaded that every clear-sighted American mind, that looks with a comprehensive glance at the condition of Europe at this moment, must have come to this conviction. If this be admitted, then the other conviction must follow: that all the populations of the secondary, dependent states of the continent have a right to belong to nationalities invested and empowered with all the attributes, aspects, faculties, and dignities of independent sovereignty. And to these they never can attain until they shall be willing and able to become part of a great whole, instead of continuing, what they are, the whole of a little nothing. In a word, we believe that if all the states on the continent of Europe were united so as to form but *three* great nationalities, a vast political gain would accrue to each and all. And why should that social attraction which has already united so many distinct communities in Christendom, cease to operate until it has produced this great result? Look at it territorially. The whole of Europe, continent and island, contains about 3,500,000 square miles, or an area but a little larger than that of the United States. Now are not *four* independent nations enough to occupy this space? What American citizen could fancy that the territory of the Union could sustain advantageously more than *four* distinct governments, were it to be divided into different states? What is there in the land-area of continental Europe that renders it less integral, compact, or coherent than that of the United States. The Mediterranean makes for it a continuous, well-defined boundary on the south. The Baltic certainly projects a tongue of sea for a long distance through the northern portion of the continent; but this does not break up its compactness and continuity, any more than Lake Michigan does to the territory of the United States, in partially separating Illinois from Michigan. The voyage from Buffalo to Cleveland, or from Cleveland to Detroit, is about as long as the passage between Kiel and Copenhagen, or between Stettin and the Swedish coast. Denmark and Sweden are no more widely separated from Germany than is Ireland or Jersey from Great Britain. In fact, the Baltic, in a certain sense, makes the continent more *one* in continuity than it would do if it were a range of mountains or a plain of sand. It is a high-road of commerce and communication between the countries it nominally divides, and tends to unite them more closely than all the railroads in the world could unite Belgium and Hungary. But while the Senators and Representatives of California are virtually obliged to make two sea-voyages as far as from New York to St. Petersburgh, in order to reach Washington, no American mind, we are confident, will perceive, for a moment, any barrier in the narrow Baltic to a legislative union of Denmark and Sweden with Germany; or, at least, no interruption in the oneness of the European continent. It cannot, surely, be necessary to dwell longer on its *territorial* adaptation to that union of nationalities which we are considering.

The next point in natural order of consideration is that of *population*. Would the two hundred and thirty-five millions of inhabitants of Europe be too large a number to be divided among *four* nationalities? That is the question, pure and simple, under this head of our investigation. Russia has already one-fourth of all these souls, *numerically;* which is really the poorest aspect of their political value. Would it be dangerous or impracticable for Germany and France to have each nearly as many as Russia? Are fifty millions of men, women, and children too large a number of human beings to live under one government, however well constituted? too large for an autocracy, a democracy, or a constitutional monarchy? too large for the American Republic?

There are thousands living in the United States who were fathers or mothers when the whole population of the Union did not number *four* millions. They have lived to see it six times that number. It doubled itself between 1830 and 1850. This they saw with their own eyes. Then will not their children probably see it doubled again between 1850 and 1880? And is it an extravagant estimate to suppose that, in less than fifty years from the present moment, the population of the Union will reach one hundred millions? Does any American fear that all these human beings may not live harmoniously and advantageously under our republican system of government, after slavery shall have been abolished with its antagonisms? Does any American heart entertain the idea that the mere continuous peopling of the continent from Maine to Oregon is going to dissolve the Union? Surely not. Who will despair of the Republic when it shall contain one hundred millions of inhabitants? Then we are equally confident that few of our readers would deem it impracticable for fifty millions to live comfortably under the government of France or of Germany, if it were rightly administered, and made to represent and promote their interests. We will assume that this matter of mere population does not present any serious obstacle to that annexation of conterminous states proposed. Let us, then, pass on to another point, which may present, to many minds, far more difficulty than those we have already considered. We mean, the *Physiology of Nationalities.*

Having taken it for granted, that the extent of territory and the number of its inhabitants present no serious objection to this union of the continental states of Europe in three nations, let us consider next the question, what political affinities might facilitate the process and determine the boundary of such confederation We will not now go over the arguments which we have elsewhere adduced, in reference to the territory of a nation, to its integrity, compactness, right of way to the sea, the ownership of rivers, and other physical advantages of almost vital importance to its well-being. Assuming that the continental states of Europe might be reduced, by confederation, to three great nations, so far as extent of territory and population merely are concerned, then *contermineity* and commercial considerations would render it desirable that Holland, Belgium, Spain, and Portugal should be united with France, and form with it one confederate nationality. This would give it a continuous sea-coast as a northern, western, and southern boundary, and a territory of four hundred and thirty-eight thousand square miles, or a little more than one-eighth of that of the United States, and an aggregate population of about sixty millions. The same circumstances that make this arrangement desirable and convenient, would render it equally advantageous to unite Denmark, Sweden, Norway, Switzerland, and the whole of Italy with Germany. This would give to the confederate nation virtually as much sea-coast as France would possess, and equal facilities for foreign commerce and maritime enterprise. It would have the Mediterranean for its southern boundary, and for its pathway to the Atlantic. On the north, it would have both coasts of the Baltic and its ports on either side, together with the ocean coast of Norway and Denmark. The whole territory and population would be larger than France would have under its jurisdiction; but in fertility of soil, compactness of area, and intelligence of people, the latter would always be quite equal to its great neighbour-nation. Thus Germany would extend from the Northern Ocean to the Mediterranean, embracing the islands in that sea. Then all eastward of her eastern boundary, within the limits of Europe, should belong to Russia; that is, European Turkey, Greece, and the Danubian Principalities. This would give that nation a commercial base on the Mediterranean, and two free pathways, through that sea and the Baltic, to the Atlantic.

Admitting that the States of Continental Europe may be confederated in *three* nations, our readers will perhaps concede that the arrangement we have suggested would be the most proper and practicable. We now come to the consideration of an obstacle to this extensive annexation of States, which to many may seem insuperable or extremely difficult. That is, the amalgamation of different races under one government. To an American mind that dwells with satisfaction upon the energy and enterprise that have peopled the North

American continent with a mighty nation in the memory of the living, this question of amalgamation cannot present a serious objection to the plan proposed. Those remarkable qualities which distinguish the American people and enable them to achieve what they do by land and sea, they have derived from one of the most extraordinary amalgamations of races that ever took place on the surface of the globe. We have already found in the history of England one of the most striking instances of the union of antagonistic, sensitive, jealous nationalities. From the same history we may derive the most illustrious and conclusive proof not only of the possibility, but of the immeasurable advantage, of amalgamating, under one government, the most antagonistic races of men. We say, immeasurable advantage, and that is not saying enough—the vital, indispensable necessity of such amalgamation. Not for physical characteristics or capacities merely is it indispensable, but for the highest moral attributes that can distinguish a nation. Nay, more, one might venture to affirm, that no primitive or elementary race of men have ever been able to attain to a full capacity of self-government, even if they have been able to maintain an independent nationality; and it is doubtful whether such a people will ever alone reach this capacity. Look at the combination of races on the island of Great Britain and its result. The most hostile and dissimilar in blood, religion, and language were brought together on that small sea-girt territory. First were the aboriginal Britons—or that Celtic element which was the common and primitive *stratum* not only of Great Britain, but of France, Spain, and other countries. Then the Romans came and prepared this foundation element for fusion with another race of far higher qualities, if they did not amalgamate with the British Celts themselves. Next came the blue-eyed, light-haired Saxons, with their plastic moral natures; with their capacity of patience, suffering, hope, and love of *home*, of quiet, of peaceful agriculture, of thatched cottages with birds' nests in their gables. What elements to bring together! The Celts and Saxons! Where in Europe could be found races more dissimilar and mutually antagonistic, to all human seeming? What wonder that centuries elapsed before these two elements were harmoniously combined, even in England proper? At the right stage of the combination came another people—the Danes—and added a new and vigorous element, a hardy daring, a maritime genius, a boundless propensity for seafaring enterprise and adventure. This element was almost entirely wanting in the Saxons, and it gave to them a new life and history. As soon as this amalgamation was effected, the Normans came with their higher civilization, with their architectural and mechanical genius, their arts, habits, aristocratic ways and notions, and other surface-qualities of show and seeming, their learning and literature, and a good deal of mercurial impetuosity of temper. These Norman qualities, though wanting many vital ingredients in themselves, when blended with the combined elements they found in England, produced the most extraordinary race on the face of the globe. In every country, climate, and condition it retains and shows the vitality of each of its component elements, and the result of their combination. Everywhere it presents its Saxon, Danish, and Norman features. Everywhere it takes to the land with all the farming and rural predilections of the Saxons in the ninth century. Everywhere it takes to the water with all the duck-like propensities of the Danes in the tenth century. Everywhere it takes to all the manufacturing and mechanical industry, to all the architectural taste, embellishment, elegant show and enjoyment that marked the Normans in the twelfth century.

So much for the *mental* constitution of the Anglo-Saxon race, resulting from the amalgamation we have described. Look at the *physical* qualities and characteristics it derives from the same combination. It *quadruples* itself where any other race *doubles* its population. Look at one simple fact, and appreciate its significance. In 1800, the population of France was twenty-seven millions. The whole population of the Anglo-Saxon race in that year, in Great Britain, Ireland, the British Colonies, and the United States did not number twenty-five millions. At the present moment, it cannot fall much short of seventy millions, occupying nearly all the islands and continents of the globe. While France has gained only about eight millions from 1800, the race to which we belong has increased in population by forty-five millions! With the development of Australia and of the vast continent of North America, there is no reason to doubt that this race will *treble* itself in the next half-century, or number two hundred millions in 1900.

But these physical and mental capacities and characteristics are not the principal results which we would adduce in favour of that amalgamation of races involved in the union of European States. The most important advantage they would derive from it would be a capacity for self-government and civil freedom to which they have not yet attained, and which it may be doubted that they will ever attain without such amalgamation. We hope no accidental reader will be offended at the view which we venture to present, or deem it an invidious distinction, if we say that it is hopeless to expect any high attainment of civil liberty in a nation which has not a large infusion of the *Saxon* element. A thousand years' experience justifies this conclusion, and removes it from the category of theory. But in face of this experience, no element of national population has been treated with more indignity than the Saxon, and by those who most needed it to lift them from an ignoble political condition. The Celtic families of Europe have always manifested a great repugnance to the Saxon. How seemingly implacable has been the hostility of the Irish Celts! How they have recoiled from amalgamation with their "natural enemy," as they call him. All the proud, fiery races, with their mercurial temperaments, have affected to despise the patient, plastic, home-loving, hopeful Saxon. The Normans despised him, and tried to make him their beast of burden. Proud Castilians despise him still, while they themselves are perishing from the earth for lack of his very qualities. The haughty, aristocratic *Magyars* found him obnoxious to their Asiatic instincts. To the Polish nation of nobles and serfs he was equally repugnant. If those classes in Hungary and Poland who think they were born to own and rule the common people, had their way, they would probably drive out the Saxon from their borders. But for all this, he is the most essential to the races which most obstinately reject him. Without that element which his constitution imparts, they cannot rise to the full stature of national independence and civil freedom. They may revolutionize, upset thrones, defeat armies, build barricades, and fill the world with the brilliance of burning eloquence. They may frame paper constitutions, and head them with grand preambles of patriotism. But all this cannot establish liberty. All this cannot safely helm the ship of civil state against the leeward drift and the stress and strain and counter-currents of passion. Look at the history of France. What nation has been more frequently and deeply convulsed by struggles for liberty? For a brief space they seem to have attained it, in its largest circumference and prerogative. But soon they fall back. They lack that steadfast, conservative element of character which will hold fast what is gained. In a word, they lack the Saxon. Look at Spain, at home and abroad, in all the countries which it has colonized, and in which its race and language exist. See how it is for ever alternating between anarchy and despotism. It lacks the Saxon. Look at Poland; turn over the pages of its history of internal confusion, violence, and corruption for five hundred years. If fiery bravery, and the heroics of martial spirit and prowess, and other qualities held up to our admiration, could have sustained their nationality, it would now be ranked with the independent Powers of Europe. They lacked the Saxon, its capacity of conservative patience, self-control, hope, and faith in the power of moral virtues and plodding industry. Look at Hungary and its history. Study the qualities of the lauded Magyar race and its *magnates*. Admit all their innate pride and independence of spirit; their noble bearing; their feeling of superiority to all other races in the country ; their habit and aptitude for ruling; their fiery courage and inflammable enthusiasm. Admit the existence in them of all these qualities, for which we are expected to admire their name, and you have precisely those characteristics which produce and mark despotism and anarchy in their periodical alternations. They lack in their moral

and political constitution what they affect most to despise
—the *Saxon;* and without the infusion of that element
we see no prospect of their ever attaining to that condition of freedom to which we all desire they may be
raised. We would not have a nation all *Saxon*, any
more than a man all *heart*, without genius or intellect.
Germany has too much Saxon; therefore we would infuse
into it the vivacity and glow of the Italians, the ruder
vehemence of the Magyars, and the hardy maritime
genius of the Scandinavians. France has too little
Saxon by far to render it capable of the highest stage of
self-government; we would therefore amalgamate with
her all the Saxon or German element west of the Rhine,
and the staid Belgians and phlegmatic Dutch, together
with the Spanish and Portuguese nations.

It would be easy to bring forward other advantages
resulting from the reduction of the nominally independent States of Continental Europe to three great
and equal nationalities. The commercial benefits would
be incalculable. Then the great expense of sustaining
a large number of national Governments and establishments would be saved to the people of Europe. The
subject of one Government would be invested with the
same political value and influence as the subject of any
other. His nation would be equal in power and dignity
to any of the three European Powers. There would be
no more battle-grounds of foreign diplomacy contending
for supremacy of influence over a secondary State. The

Balance-of-Power Question would be solved for ever, and removed as a source of suspicion and hostility. And, over and above all, the people of Continental Europe would be put on the high road to freedom by that amalgamation of races which would give them new vigour and capacity for progress.

In review of the points adduced, we are confident, that a candid American mind will see no serious obstacle to the annexation we have proposed in the character and extent of the land-area of Continental Europe, or in the number of its inhabitants. Having granted that position, we think it will be as easily admitted that the amalgamation of races involved, so far from being impracticable or impolitic, would be very desirable, and give to the confederate nations thus constructed the elements of new political life and progress. With these important considerations in favour of the arrangement, we trust it may not in the end be deemed an extravagant or untimely proposition.

—o—o—

NATIONALITY AND CIVIL FREEDOM.

WE have considered several of the aspects and bearings of nationality in its relations to the political rights and well-being of the various peoples of Christendom. We have endeavoured to show, that their interests would be greatly promoted by allowing

that law of social attraction to have its course, which
has already united so many large communities and
different races of men in one nation. We have estimated
some of the results of the working of this law, should
it continue to operate upon the different States of
Europe, until they should all gravitate into four great
Nationalities, of nearly equal population and political
status and power, or into Great Britain, France, Russia,
and Germany. It has been assumed that no American
mind, at least, would regard the present or prospective
number of the inhabitants of Europe as too large to be
divided among four nations. We have taken it for
granted, that there is nothing in the extent or character
of the territory of Europe that would render such
a division dangerous or impracticable; that there is
nothing in the diversity of race, language, or temperament
that would make the proposed union undesirable; that
it would raise all the populations of Europe to a political
equality, to an equal value and dignity, so far as mem-
bership of equal and independent sovereignties could
impart the sentiment and establish the condition of
parity; that it would relieve them of the devouring
expense of sustaining so many national establishments;
that it would infuse into races or communities degraded
by centuries of oppression a new and elevating element;
that it would Saxonize fiery and mercurial temperaments,
and thus impart a capacity of self-government to populations which have oscillated between the wild anarchy

of their own passions and that despotism which is everywhere and for ever the reaction of anarchy; that on the
other hand, it would infuse into the rather lymphatic
temperament of the great German or Teutonic family a
little of the fire and vivacity of the Magyar and Italian
constitutions, thus receiving the impulse of progress from
races to which in return it communicated the conser-
vatism of hope, patience, reason, and faith.

What possible result, then, could be reasonably apprehended from the proposed union, which would be
detrimental to any people in Europe? Would it impede
or peril the progress of civil freedom in any country on
that continent? Would the people of Spain lose any
thing by being associated with the patient, plodding,
slowly, but surely, progressing Dutch, as equal States of
one great empire, whose helm of nationality should be in
Paris? Would Naples be retarded in its progress by
being connected with Norway, under one great Imperial
Government, whose centre should be Frankfort-on-the-
Maine? Would European Turkey and its various races
hazard any capacity or prospect of advancement in
civilization and liberty by forming an equal part with
the Russian provinces of one grand nationality, having
its seat of government at Moscow? Would Athens
lose any political dignity by being thus associated with
Odessa, or Constantinople by being put on the same
footing as St. Petersburgh?

To the American or English mind, the question,

how the union of European Nationalities would affect
the progress of popular freedom, must naturally and
inevitably be the first and foremost to be considered.
All other considerations must sink into comparative
insignificance, when put in the balance against this
vital question. In this country, especially, national independence and civil freedom mean one and the same
thing, in popular estimation. They meant one and the
same thing at the beginning of the American Revolution; and through all that long and desperate struggle,
they retained that precious significance. To build up a
new nationality in this Western World was not the great
purpose of the fathers of the Republic, but to raise
man, as an individual, to the full stature of his inalienable rights; to enable him to stand forth in the strength
and symmetry of civil liberty; free to worship GOD
according to the dictates of his own conscience; free
in the pursuit of happiness; equal before every law of
the land; equally eligible to the first place in its government; participating with a vote of equal value in its
legislation. The very heart of American patriotism
clings, with all its life-strings, to national independence
as the only source and guaranty of these political rights
and dignities of man as an individual. What wonder,
then, that the American mind should embrace the
idea, that national independence everywhere means civil
freedom? that in every struggle to raise up a fallen
nationality in Europe, no other aspiration or aim is

recognized than that of elevating the political condition of man, of giving him the value and dignity which are his due? This idea is spontaneous and natural. If it errs it errs on the virtuous and hopeful side of human judgment and sympathy. And erred it has, and widely, in connexion with many a struggle waged in the name of civil liberty. In its generous and unsuspecting charity, it has believed that, to erect an independent nationality was to erect a free man; to recognize and establish his inalienable rights. Now a few simple facts should suffice to show that this hopeful impression is as mistaken as it is generous; that national independence and civil freedom may be as far apart as the poles in their aims and relations. Still the public mind both in the United States and England seems almost blind to a perception of this difference. In both countries, independent nationality appears to be regarded as the only embodiment of popular rights, and the only condition to which patriotism should aspire. So complete and universal is this conclusion, that the condition of the mass of the people is almost entirely overlooked. Thus the struggle of the renowned Schamyl and his fierce Circassian clan to hold their mountain fastnesses and their national independence, commands a lively sympathy, as a struggle for liberty, for the rights of man. Yet, one of the rights which the Circassian seems most to value, is that of selling his own children to the highest bidder, and of stealing his neighbour's for the same market. The

U

question, whether the moral and political condition of the subjects of this little pagan despotism would not be greatly improved by their being brought under a Government which would abolish these inhuman practices, rarely if ever enters into the popular estimate of the protracted contest. Public sympathy is thus concentrated upon the governing class, not the governed. Its pulses all throb and palpitate in behalf of the image of the nation, not for the image of GOD; not for the individual man and his birth-right prerogatives. As a striking illustration of this misdirection of sympathy, both in the United States and in England, look at its outflow in the case of Poland. The tears which fall at its unhappy fate should not blind our eyes to the fact, that national independence and civil freedom were never more widely severed in Christendom than in the history of that unfortunate country. At the time of its fall, no State in Europe had run a wilder career of anarchy and despotism; or shown a greater want of public virtue, or trampled with more ruthless contempt upon the inherent rights of man. By no State pretending to civilization had the cause of popular liberty been more deeply outraged, in form and principle. Two great vital evils ate slowly into the heart of the nation, filled its veins with corruption, paralysed the nerves of its political being; and it fell. No alliance or aid of neighbouring Powers could have held it up in the posture of a living State. From the first to the last day of its probation, through all

its various stages and phases of violence and demoralization, one small governing class constituted the nation,
and ruled it with a senseless and fanatic tyranny, to
which a parallel could hardly be found in the annals of
modern history. They not only grasped and exercised
the whole power and authority of the State, but de-
moralized the people whom they disfranchised and
oppressed by their own lawless license and lack of good
faith and patriotism. A distinguished German writer,
describing the condition of Poland under this sway of
anarchy, remarks: "Never was the corruption of a
State so fearful as here, where the nobility constituted the
nation." An eminent British statesman thus sums up
the character of this turbulent and despotic oligarchy:
"Down to the partition of their territory, about nineteen out of every twenty of the inhabitants were slaves,
possessing no rights civil or political. About one in
every twenty was a nobleman; and this body of noble-
men formed the very worst aristocracy in ancient or
modern times, putting up and pulling down their kings
at pleasure; passing selfish laws, which gave them the
power of life and death over their serfs, whom they
bought and sold like dogs and horses; usurping to each
of themselves the privileges of a petty sovereign, and
denying to all besides the meanest rights of human
beings; and, scorning all pursuits as degrading, except
that of the sword, they engaged in incessant wars with
neighbouring States, or they plunged their country into

all the horrors of anarchy, for the purpose of giving employment to themselves and their descendants!" Count Garowski, a Polish nobleman, who took an active part in the Revolution of 1831, in a work upon his native country quite recently published, confirms and extends this view, in the following language: "The reckless, ungovernable and egotistical spirit of the nobility destroyed Poland beyond recovery and caused her death.

* * * * * * * * *

The Polish nobility, from the first moment of their political existence, appear most jealous of the privileges of caste, destroying political life in all other parts of the nation. After having enslaved the people or peasants, they deprived the burghers and cities of their political franchise. In the sixteenth century, the deputies of cities were formally and for ever expelled from the assemblies of the National Diet."

Such was the condition of the great mass of the inhabitants of Poland at the time of its partition. However we may condemn the flagrant iniquity of that act, they lost not one iota of civil freedom or political dignity by it. That portion of the population transferred to Prussia gained immeasurably. The portion that fell to Russia found their condition greatly improved even by its stern but steady rule. They must see and feel that the chance of final emancipation is far greater under that Government than it would have been under the relentless power of the Polish oligarchy which had robbed them for generations of every civil and political right. We believe that no one will dispute that it is a feature of the Russian system, to put the people of the countries brought under its sway upon an equal footing with the inhabitants of the original provinces of the Empire. In some cases a kind of favouritism is manifested towards these annexed populations, to attach them, it is said, more closely to the Imperial Government. Lord John Russell, in his memorable speech in Parliament, after his return from Vienna, speaking of the power of Russia in Poland, says, " She has conciliated the peasantry by a policy artfully adapted to that purpose." What policy, and how adapted to this end? Undoubtedly a system of amelioration of their condition and prospects; inspiring them with the hope of being freed from the serfdom to which they and their ancestors have been subjected so long; and placing them on the high-road of progress to all the privileges that can be reached and enjoyed by any population in the Russian Empire. If then we do not recognize the little oligarchy that ruled and ruined Poland as constituting the Polish nation, we must admit that the cause of civil freedom lost nothing by the partition of that country between neighbouring States; and that it would gain nothing by that " Restoration " which has excited so much sympathy on both sides of the Atlantic. It is very doubtful whether even the resident nobility of Poland would gain anything by this Restoration. It would not satisfy their old lust of power. All could not sit on the throne or stand at the helm of State at once. Whether King or President, but one of their number could fill that post of honour at one time; and the subordinate offices would not be much more numerous than those accessible in the country under the present rule. Independent nationality would not, therefore, make places in Poland for all its native nobility ambitious to govern for their personal distinction and power. Their chance for such honours would, on the contrary, be much diminished; for they would be confined entirely within the bounds of Poland, while if faithful to Russia, they might have the range of all the offices in the gift of the Czar, within the compass of that vast empire. Those of their number who have given in their full adhesion to that Power have been equally eligible, with Russian-born nobles, to the posts of honour which it has created. One of the sources of the strength of that Government has been the policy of disregarding both rank and race, and consulting only personal merit and fitness, in filling the most important and distinguished places of trust. Thus, in a word, we cannot see how the national independence of Poland would either promote the civil freedom of the mass of its inhabitants, or even satisfy the ambition of its old governing nobility for glory, honour, and power. The Revolution of 1831 was evidently a struggle on the part of this aristocratic class to restore their nationality, and their old relations to the common people, not to elevate them to the dignity and rights of civil citizenship. The common people or the peasantry understood this, and resisted the re-erection of a nationality which, they apprehended, would inevitably reduce them to that old condition of oppression from which they had been raised by Russian rule. In their view, national independence would be to them a hopeless subjugation to the sway of that oligarchy which they and their ancestors had served in the bitterest serfdom.

If we divest our minds of the influence of that admiration and sympathy which the Hungarian Revolution inspired throughout most of Christendom, and look at it dispassionately, we shall find that it was far more a struggle for national independence than for civil freedom. In Hungary, the Magyar nobility, a proud, fierce, fiery aristocracy, had governed for centuries. For a thousand years they had retained their Asiatic instincts, and the lowest of their rank felt himself " born to command." For a thousand years they had lived with the races which they had subjugated without amalgamating with them. Never constituting much more than one-third of the population of the country, the Magyars were lords of the soil, as well as rulers; and the vassalage to which they reduced the other inhabitants was as severe and humiliating as possible. But, what added a peculiar sting to this humiliation, was the aggravating circumstance, that the Magyar magnates or masters ruled as conquerors over races more numerous than their own,

and which they treated as if only born and fitted for
servitude. These smothered jealousies and animosities
rendered the work of reform all the more difficult in
Hungary. But there was an enlightened nobleman found
to lead the way in this arduous enterprise, supported by
other eminent men. Count Stephen Széchényi headed
this patriotic movement, and gave to it devotion and
practical talent which should command the veneration of
every friend of freedom. Owing chiefly to his indefatigable activity, says an English writer, "feudal vassalage
was for ever abolished; all classes, of whatever race—
whether Magyar, Croat, Serb, or Wallach—since elevated to the dignity of freemen; the rights and privileges
of the small landed proprietors specifically defined; and
various reforms introduced indispensable to the well-
being of the people. In addition to this, all religions
were tolerated; neither did the profession of any creed
whatever incapacitate a man from holding the highest
offices of the State. To a traveller like ourselves, who
remembered a country destitute of roads, rivers without
bridges, peasants half-naked, towns and cities unpaved
and unlighted, huts built of wood or mud, barges labori-
ously drawn by degraded serfs, the improved condition
of everything that now met our view, seemed like the
realization of a fairy tale. Pesth, Buda, Presburg, and
all the other great towns and cities could boast of
palaces and public buildings which would be admired
for the beauty of their architecture even in the meridian

of London and Paris. Stagnant moats, which shed around their pestilential exhalations, were filled up and converted into public promenades. A magnificent suspension bridge, thrown across the Danube, connected Pesth with Buda, while hospitals and benevolent institutions richly endowed had been established to relieve the wants of the poorer part of the population. If we penetrated into the rural districts, they also exhibited all the indications of prosperity — comfortable farmhouses, villages, and road-side inns everywhere meet the view, together with an improved system of agriculture. At the same time, the number of steamboats that kept moving to and fro on the bosom of the mighty Danube, the Save, and the Theiss, carrying the produce of the country into foreign lands, and returning with the manufactures and luxuries of France and Great Britain, gave evidence of the increasing wealth and prosperity of the country. Having succeeded in breaking down all the barriers that existed between the noble and the peasant, in abrogating all the feudal rights and privileges enjoyed by the former, Count Széchényi extorted from the Emperor of Austria, as King of Hungary, the recognition of the constitutional rights and independence of his country."

Such is the picture drawn by an English traveller of the improvement wrought in Hungary, chiefly through the exertions of one devoted reformer. All these most important steps towards the highest condition of civil freedom had been achieved when this writer visited the country in 1847, or before the struggle for national independence. These vital rights and institutions had been obtained in the course of a few years. A separate nationality was evidently not necessary for their acquisition. Had Kossuth given his magnificent abilities to the work of man-raising, instead of nation-building, not only the people of his beloved country, but all the varied populations of the Austrian Empire would doubtless have this day been lifted, if not to the summit level of civil liberty, at least to a high position in the ranks of freedom.

The rights of man, his value, his dignity, and destiny, are just as precious in Bohemia as in Hungary; in Muscovy as in Poland. Man was born before nationalities. His rights were written by the finger of GOD on the charter of his being before human governments existed. First among the entities of humanity is man with his birth-right dignities. For one, looking at the centuries of his history, we see his immortal value frittered away in the current estimate of institutions. He is governed too much in Europe. We long to see more men and fewer nations on that continent. Therefore we hope that the force of social attraction which has already drawn together so many European States, will not cease in its operation until all the populations of that quarter of the globe shall be divided among four great nationalities.

Thoughts at the Plough.

"NOW, if you want to exercise yourself in the farming line, why didn't you go and buy three or four rich, level, mellow acres and till them garden-fashion, instead of purchasing that stony, poverty-stricken hill?" So asked one of our friends, with a severe wonderment of manner, which showed that the question was not for information, but to convey reproof interrogatively. A near neighbour, in stout overalls, passing by with a long whiplash at the masthead, stood up in his ox-cart and pitched over the wall upon us this serious and suggestive salutation, as we were tugging at a great bottle-bottomed boulder: "Look here, neighbour, you'll want to get your life insured, if you think of clearing off all them rocks and stones." Another good old-fashioned farmer, with a barnyard full of cattle and sheep and pigs, encourages our undertaking after this wise: "You can never do anything with that land; you never can bring it up to any heart; all you put on it will leak through like sand in a sieve." These admonitions are the best meant in the world, and worthy of thoughtful consideration. Such we give them. They are impressive, and come with the weight of three generations' experience,

to our certain knowledge. This very little hill, so barren,
so covered with mossgrown stones, so pale with sickly
daisies in summer, so black with their decaying stalks in
autumn, is a proof presumptive that it has been given
over to waste for a hundred years. In itself no great
loss has come to the community from this neglect. But
New England is studded with a hundred thousand of
such hills. Old Connecticut wears at least ten thousand
in the necklace with which Nature bedecked her as a
dowry of healthful and virtuous benefactions. There
never would have been any New England at all, in
moral or distinctive characteristics, were it not for her
hills. Suppose her whole territory had been a great
Illinois prairie—flat, fat, fertile, and feverish. What
then? Here is our argument and apology for undertaking to clear away the stones and briars from this
carbuncle in Nature's belt, and to put a new face upon
it in spring and summer. First, a sense of what we
owe as a people to these neglected hills blends with
this work. Then there is another feeling perhaps more
ambitious and questionable. There would be no merit
in growing corn, rye, and potatoes down yonder in the
mellow acres of the valley. Nature would carry off
seventy-five per cent. of the honour of the crop. But
here, reverently be it said, we can go in copartnership
with Divine Providence in the work of creation. To
improve on the maxim of the French monarch, and
make even two spires of grass grow where one didn't

before, is as near an approach to the work of creation as man can well make in this world. Then there is the gratification of taste—taste for landscape painting. Some rich men will pay several thousand dollars for a contracted glimpse of natural scenery transferred to canvas, and looking as lifelike as a stuffed bird with glass eyes. With what pride and pleasure he hangs up the picture in its gilt frame against the wall of his choicest room! But compare his costly picture with the glorious panorama of living and speaking scenery painted by Nature from this hill. This, then, is our picture, worth all we paid for the gallery to see it from. Instead of hanging the painting against a parlour wall, we intend to hang the wall, if we ever build one, against the painting. There is another thought enlisted in the enterprise. The recovery of this hill to beautiful verdure and profitable production may lead others to similar works of re-creation, until "cattle upon a thousand hills" may be a positive and extensive reality in hitherto sterile portions of the State, and not a figure of speech, merely applying to distant countries. Cattle indeed! why the most stinted race of sheep could hardly grub up a living upon half the hills in Connecticut. Take care of the hills, say we, and the valleys will take care of themselves. Our fingers, with the blessing of Providence, are to make this on which we daily toil as green as any of our neighbours', in two or three years. There is a challenge for you. Let us to the work. We never saw a town on either side of the

Atlantic girdled with such a noble belt of hills as this, including Kensington. The gracious and rich economies of Nature and Providence will do their part, depend on it. Let us, then, make this belt a string of emeralds instead of red clay beads.

—◦—◦—

THE DIGNITY OF THE FARMER'S OCCUPATION.

IT is not with the enthusiasm of an amateur or novice that we think these thoughts about farming; its dignity, poetry, and patriotism. They come out of long and mature reflection on human occupations, their moral tendencies and results. If they are correct, we wish every man and boy who follows the plough would make them his own. Persons in certain professions or businesses are full of what the French call *esprit de corps*. They pride themselves on the dignity of their occupation. There is the banker: see with what self-complacency and self-estimation he stands behind the cashier's desk, or in the director's chair, and decides like a grave judge upon the value and discountability of that I. O. U., handed over with timorous deference and trembling expectancy by a small trader, manufacturer, or farmer. With what a grace-dispensing air the money is counted out to the applicant, as if the ten or twelve per cent.

charged him did not diminish his debt of humble gratitude for such a dispensation. There are the three-graded
merchants — the importer, factor, and retailer. Every
mother's son of them is full of the spirit of his order,
and prides himself on the rank of his position. In all
countries, the aristocratic vein of feeling runs through
the sentiment of their profession. In the aristocracy of
trade, the importers are the dukes, the factors the earls,
and the retailers the gentry of the order. You will find
traces of this sentiment and deportment in the smallest
log-cabin grocery in Nebraska as well as in the largest
marble-palace warehouse in New York. So it is with
manufacturers, shipowners, and other business leaders of
the land.

We are not going to find fault with this ambitious
spirit and animating sense of dignity which pervade the
classes we have mentioned. But we do say that no
class of men on earth have a better right to a distinctive
esprit de corps, and a sense of the dignity of their occupation, than the owners and tillers of the soil. To say
that, humanly speaking, they stand at the fountain-head
of all sustenance for man and beast; that they are the
bankers GOD has chosen for discounting food, and
the raw materials of raiment and shelter to all the
millions of his children upon the earth, may sound like
an old and hackneyed truism. To say that the productions of their industry constitute the prime values of the
world's wealth, and that without them diamonds would

be of no more worth than common pebbles, would be
to run into questions of political economy; and we do
not wish to run in that direction just now. But there
is a sentiment that becomes the honest and industrious
farmer; not an idle pride of order, but a grateful and
gladdening appreciation of the dignity of his occupation;
of its elevating tendencies and surroundings. There are
but three poets in the family of mankind, using that
term in its literal, Greek significance, or that which con-
veys the idea of creating. If the intelligent, cultivated
farmer is not the first, he is not the last of the trio.
What the word-poet does with the spoken language of
thought, he does with the physical syllables of creation,
or its green acres given to man. Take the grandest
epic of any language or age, and place it side by side
with the great agricultural poem of the American continent; contrast the prose material of the one with the
prose material of the other; take the elements that
Homer had ready prepared for his pen, and those which
the American farmer had for his plough, and then compare the merits of the two superstructures, and say
which of the two epic poems should rank first in estimation. The painter is a poet, in this literal signification,
because he can create, as well as imitate a landscape.
But what he can do on canvas with his pencil, the farmer
can do with his plough on the broad earth. The best
colours of the rainbow, the softest, choicest dews that
come down out of heaven, sunbeams, moonbeams, and

starbeams, and balmy south blowings, summer showers
and lightning, come and commingle on his easel of themselves, and make a picture of his cornfields that the
painter, of the oil and distilled-drug order, cannot rival.
Look at Old England. There is landscape painting for
you, that will beat Landseer's "all hollow"—the painting
of the plough done with artistic touches of exquisite
beauty. Look at that hill declining so gently into the·
meadow, with its grass so green, soft, and silky that
the great pied cows are mirrored in it more distinctly
than in water. What was that hill, we ask, three
centuries ago? What was it before the artistry of the
farmer's strong, broad hand touched it with his toil?
Crowned with coarse furze, ferns, or bushes, doubtless
the lair of reptiles or noisome vermin. Is it not a
painting now, of as fine order of genius as ever hung in
a national gallery? See those green hedges running
over it from base to base, blooming and breathing with
sweetbriar blossoms and hawthorn flowers. See the
grouping and contrast of colours, of light and shade,
which those fields present. There is one of wheat yel-
lowing to harvest. How the vivid greenness of the next
of oats contrasts with it! Next comes one in fallow,
with its lake-coloured furrows lying as even and as
straight as if turned by machinery. Then we have a
field of barley, and one of English beans, all in their
gorgeous flower; then the meadow, with its tall grass so
thick, soft and green; then the pasture descending to

the stream in the valley. Every one of these fields, surrounded by its hawthorn hedge, looks like a framed landscape painting, hung against that hill by an artist, in a way to make the whole a gallery of living pictures, arranged to show their contrasts with the greatest effect upon the traveller. Old England is one continuous gallery of this agricultural artistry; and she will doubtless, for centuries to come, be the normal school for the education of landscape painters with the plough. There is no country in the world that can be made more picturesque by the artistry of agriculture than New England, notwithstanding our long winters. In no country, not in England, at least, are the hills more grand and varied, and the valleys more extensive and adapted to a greater diversity of vegetation. Now in all this we would not advocate picture farming, or the collocation of crops merely to produce an artistic effect; or a landscape painting, which people passing may stop to admire. No farmer in England ever did that, or thought of it. All this scenic effect there is merely an incidental result of profitable industry. It comes from that rotation of crops which pays best. It is a gratuitous drapery of beauty which Nature throws around the best cultivated fields, as a token of her approbation and copartnership. "Blessed is the man who, passing through the valley of Baca, maketh it a well," saith the word of divine inspiration. Blessed, say we, is the man who, dwelling on a small allotment of the world's wilderness, maketh it to blossom as the rose; who reclaims one hill or valley acre from waste, and makes it beautiful with the verdure of grain or grass for man or beast.

—o—o—

THE FARMER'S LUXURIES.

TALK of epicures! of broiled woodcock, and pies of pheasant tongues! What is all that, with its highest seasoning, compared with the relish with which three hours' mowing has seasoned those bits of common food to that ruddy-browed farmer and his sons! The ambrosia of the idle deities of Olympus was mere pea-soup compared with the dainty of brown bread to the man who grows and eats it by the sweat of his brow. It is in this seasoning of toil that Nature and Providence bless the humblest food to the farmer with a relish unknown to the epicures of royal courts.

Drink is it? juleps, nectarine punches, and other artistic mixtures to delight the taste? Look into that deep, dark well, with the cold water just perceptible. That is a more delicious drink to the farmer than was ever distilled from nectar for Jupiter. He wants no golden or silver goblet to drink it from. The old oaken bucket, swinging on its iron swivel, is better to him than all the chased ware of luxury. See him at the windlass or the well-sweep, with his face red and dusty, and his mouth and eyes chafed with hay seed, and his throat dry with thirst. Hear the big-bottomed bucket bump against the moss-covered stones as it descends. There is the splash, and the cold, gurgling sound at the filling, and now it slowly ascends, with a spray of water-drops dripping against the wall, every one giving a new edge to the farmer's thirst. There it is, standing on the curb before him, mirroring his moistened and reddened face, which bends to the draught. There is a drink for you, that Nature has distilled for the farmer's lips, the like of which fabled Olympus never knew.

So with sleep. How many thousands of men, clothed in fine linen, faring sumptuously every day in the most gorgeous abodes that wealth can furnish, would give half their fortunes for the deep enjoyment of the farmer's slumber !

—o—o—

Birmingham: Printed by Josiah Allen, jun., 9 & 10, Livery Street.

For EU product safety concerns, contact us at Calle de José Abascal, 56–1°, 28003 Madrid, Spain or eugpsr@cambridge.org.

www.ingramcontent.com/pod-product-compliance
Ingram Content Group UK Ltd.
Pitfield, Milton Keynes, MK11 3LW, UK
UKHW040617240426
470322UK00010B/175

* 9 7 8 1 1 0 8 0 3 2 6 5 0 *